Romantic Victorian Weddings

Romantic Victorian Weddings

THEN & NOW

Satenig St.Marie and Carolyn Flaherty

Dutton Studio Books   New York

(Overleaf) Victorian wedding cake by Cile Bellefleur-Burbidge
Photograph © 1991 by Douglas Christian

DUTTON STUDIO BOOKS

Published by the Penguin Group
Penguin Books USA Inc., 375 Hudson Street,
New York, New York, 10014, U.S.A.

Penguin Books Ltd, 27 Wrights Lane,
London W8 5TZ, England

Penguin Books Australia Ltd, Ringwood,
Victoria, Australia

Penguin Books Canada Ltd, 2801 John Street,
Markham, Ontario, Canada L3R 1B4

Penguin Books (N.Z.) Ltd, 182-190 Wairau Road,
Auckland 10, New Zealand

Penguin Books Ltd, Registered Offices:
Harmondsworth, Middlesex, England

First published by Dutton Studio Books, an imprint of Penguin
Books USA Inc.

First printing, February, 1992
10 9 8 7 6 5 4 3 2 1

Library of Congress
Catalog Card Number: 91-75606

Printed and bound by Dai Nippon Printing Co., Ltd., Tokyo, Japan
Book designed by Nancy Danahy

ISBN: 0-525-93307-7

**To Jerry
with love**

Satenig St.Marie

For my mother

Carolyn Flaherty

A Word of Appreciation

One of the joys of writing a book such as this is the bonds that develop with so many people who become part of the process. A word here, an inquiry there, lead to resources not even imagined when the work began. Some of the help comes from friends of long standing, some from new acquaintances who are warm, wonderful voices at the other end of the telephone. Their interest and their support are just as important as the information and the materials they so generously make available. We cherish these relationships.

Of course, none of these bonds would have become a reality if it had not been for the most important person of all, our editor, Cyril I. Nelson, who to begin with had the confidence that this book on romantic Victorian weddings should be published. He gave us both the opportunity and the incentive to make it happen.

We wish to express particular appreciation to Mary Freedman, Meg McCreery, Penny Hallgren, and all the staff at the Pequot Library in Southport, Connecticut, for the almost daily help they provided in finding books and publications, old and new, for our research, not only from their own special collection, but from all parts of the United States as well.

Joyce Mueller, a dear friend, also deserves a special word of thanks because her book, *The Marriage of Diamonds and Dolls*, which her mother had bought for her as a little girl, became one of the prime sources of information on old Victorian weddings. The book was on loan for months, referred to almost daily, and she was gracious enough not to ask to have it back until our writing was completed.

To Florence Leon, Director of The Hermitage, Mary Frezzolini, Sallie Herman, Sue Klodowski, Deb Hazzard, and the many volunteers at The Hermitage in Ho-Ho-Kus, New Jersey, we want to say "You were so gracious, so generous, so kind, and so patient." They shared their facilities and their collections to enable us to stage our own Victorian wedding breakfast to photograph for this book.

Other museum directors were a major source of help, too. Mary Grace Pettit of the Adsmore Museum in Princeton, Kentucky, shared so many different articles, materials, and family pictures as well as all the background information for the wedding of Selina Smith and John Eugene Osborn that is included in the chapter on notable weddings. And, Margaret Elinsky of the Hunter House Victorian Museum in Norfolk, Virginia, who sent copies of invitations, receipts, and other wedding memorabilia. Both of these directors are among the warm friendly voices at the other end of the telephone. Hopefully, some day we will meet face to face.

Michael Douglas, Director of the Villa Louis Historic Site in Prairie Du Chien, Wisconsin, was nice enough to have reproduced for us one of the elaborate wedding invitations from their collection; Michelle Baird Mitchener of the Heritage Programs and Museums of Independence, Missouri, sent a wealth of information on frontier weddings; Janet Burgess of the Amazon Dry Goods Co., another telephone acquaintance, gave so generously of herself in sharing information on Victorian weddings; Cleo Stiles Bryans of Tahlequah, Oklahoma, wrote pages and pages about her knowledge of frontier-wedding customs.

Among the many conversations we had with people whom we met during the course of this project, one deserves a special mention. As admirers of the books on floral arrangements by Jane Packer of London, England, we made an appointment to stop in to see her at her shop on James Street. It was a delightful visit that added one more dimension to our insights into Victorian weddings, both then and now.

No word of appreciation can be complete without one heartfelt thank you to Pegi Bernard who followed words that were written up one side of the page, down the other, in between lines and even at odd angles to type this manuscript. Not only did she manage to decipher everything, but she maintained her enthusiasm throughout. Working with her as a partner was a real joy.

Contents

IDEAS TO BORROW FROM THE PAST

ROMANTIC VICTORIAN WEDDINGS—NOW

Romantic
Victorian Weddings

+THEN+

Introduction

This book is not for brides only. It is for everyone who would like to recapture the romance of a Victorian wedding.

There's something old for those who want to know about the actual customs, traditions, fashions, and etiquette of Victorian weddings, and there's something new for those who want to plan a wedding now in the romantic Victorian tradition. There's even something sentimental for those who want to celebrate anniversaries of weddings. And for those who enjoy the pure romance of it all, there's a chapter on notable Victorian weddings, those that were impressive then as well as now, beginning with that of the one who started it all, Queen Victoria.

Although it has been carefully researched from original sources that the Victorians themselves would have turned to for advice, this book is not intended to be a scholarly presentation on Victorian weddings of the past. Instead, we selected those customs, those traditions, those details, and yes, even those superstitions from the various decades of the Victorian era that in our opinion were the most enchanting. We learned that the Victorian wedding was a sentimental occasion in which every practice was symbolic, every tradition had a purpose, and every detail had a meaning of its own.

The average Victorian wedding didn't last very long. At the most it lasted only three hours from the time the marriage ceremony began until the bride and groom left for their honeymoon, and it took only three months to plan from the time the engagement was announced to the day of the wedding. It was romantic, because each of the elements was thoughtfully planned to express the bride's sentiments about love and marriage. The orange blossoms she wore spoke of her purity; the flowers she selected for her bouquet reflected her feelings for the groom; the color theme was planned for its emotional symbolism; and young children included in the wedding party meant that she hoped the marriage would be fruitful. It was a pageant of love that the guests understood and appreciated.

It seemed to us that these same elements, borrowed from the past, could be successfully adapted to plan a sentimental wedding for the present.

So we decided to stage a Victorian wedding for this book. Our concerns were not unlike those of any prospective bride and groom. We wanted a romantic wedding in a charming setting—one that would be memorable, yet affordable. Above all, we wanted to apply all that we had learned about Victorian weddings of the past so as to create a sentimental wedding that would be right for today.

The first decision was probably the most important one: where to hold the wedding. It must be Victorian, it must be a charming setting for a very sentimental occasion, and it must have space for both the ceremony and the reception, since many Victorian weddings were held at home. We found the perfect place—The Hermitage in Ho-Ho-Kus, New Jersey—an outstanding example of a Gothic Revival Cottage, which is both a national landmark and a national historic site. It has a parlor for the wedding ceremony, a dining room for the reception and is spacious enough to accommodate between forty and eighty guests.

Next came the details: the flowers and the food. We wanted both to be authentic, and we wanted whatever was created for our "wedding" to be something that could be duplicated or adapted by anyone who wants to have a Victorian wedding. We asked Ellen Lesser, a specialist in Victorian flowers, to create all the arrangements, including some bouquets and headpieces for the bride and her attendants. She chose those varieties of plants and flowers that the Victorians themselves would have used.

For our wedding breakfast, Catherine Titus Felix, a food consultant, planned and prepared all the refreshments adapted from original menus of the past to accommodate eating patterns of the present. Catherine even designed and made the shades for the princess lamps on the buffet.

Photographs of the various components of our staged wedding have been used throughout this book. The old bridal gowns and accessories are from the extensive collection at The Hermitage.

As for some of the charming customs and traditions of the Victorian wedding, we selected those that were the most sentimental for our chapter about "Ideas to Borrow from the Past."

We defined our time frame for a Victorian wedding rather nostalgically, as being sometime during the reign of Queen Victoria (1837–1901) to sometime after the turn of the century. After all, the influence of the era did not cease the day that Victoria died, and in fact, some values that were important to that period still remain in our society today.

The second part of this book is a resource for those who want to plan a romantic wedding in the Victorian tradition. It includes a comprehensive listing of historic sites, small hotels, inns, bed and breakfasts, cottages, mansions, churches, and even a tall ship in Texas, all of which are available for weddings. We personally contacted each location and have listed only those who wished to be included.

In addition, Ellen Lesser has written a section on Victorian wedding flowers, with instructions for making the decorations she created for our wedding at The Hermitage, and Catherine Felix explains how and why she adapted the old menus and recipes, and makes suggestions for planning, preparing, and serving the refreshments for a wedding breakfast. Her part includes recipes as well as a pattern for making shades for the princess lamps used on the buffet.

Then there is advice from Janet Rigby, a specialist on old textiles, about the pros and cons of wearing a vintage wedding dress. We have also included names and addresses of experts who can restore old gowns and sources for ordering shoes, gloves, and even invitations and wedding certificates.

We tried to anticipate all the details that make a wedding romantic and then personally researched the sources.

This certainly has been an interesting experience: researching and writing a book on Victorian weddings. Reading all the old books and magazines for hours at a time, day after day, was like stepping back in time to the day before yesterday. It was a romantic experience in itself that hopefully will beckon to all who look through and read this book.

The Hermitage, Ho-Ho-Kus, New Jersey

Courtship and the Proposal

Victorian girls, from the time that they were little, had visions of becoming a bride. More than being just a dream, it was a goal, because the right marriage was one of the few ways that a woman could gain status in society.

Her family made sure that she was trained in the skills that an eligible young lady was supposed to have: needlework, painting, music, French. She was coached in all the rules of etiquette concerning the behavior of young ladies, especially when socializing with young men. By the time she had reached the age when courtship started, her grooming was ready for the real test—not just to catch a man, but to catch the right man. Ideally, he would be upright, unselfish, industrious, not poor or struggling, patient and affectionate, a man of fine ideals and genuine piety; and he would be ten years older than she.

The chances of finding a husband were not all equal. The better the quality of the education of the young lady, the less her chances of marriage. Teachers were considered especially handicapped, because they had only limited opportunity to associate with the opposite sex. Location was a major factor. The marriage rate was lowest in New England and highest in the mountain states. Idaho, in 1899, had the best ratio: 16,584 bachelors to 1426 maids. Arizona and Wyoming had the next best ratios. Even so, there had to be an approved situation in which a young man and a young lady could meet.

In the West, in the early days of the Victorian era, there was a tradition known as Bonnet Day that originated in Clay County, Missouri, in 1826. On the second Sunday in May, when presumably all the women would have acquired their new dresses and bonnets, the Big Shoal Meeting House had a full attendance at worship. The young ladies were seated on one side of the House, along with the older women, and the men on the other. During the long service, there was ample opportunity for the girls to display their charms from under the brims of their colorful new bonnets, and for the young men to decide which ones they wanted to meet. After the service, when it was perfectly respectable for everyone to socialize, they had time to flirt and become acquainted with one another, under the watchful eyes of the congregation, of course.

In the major cities, and especially in the East, there were social functions such as church suppers and holiday balls, although a gentleman who had been introduced to a lady at a ball for the purpose of dancing was not to assume that he could speak to her at another time or at

A young lady, to be eligible for marriage, was not trained in household management but rather in such skills as needlework, painting, music, and French.

some other place. It just wasn't proper. Ideally, they had to be formally introduced.

If a gentleman wished to become acquainted with a certain young lady, he had to make subtle inquiries to find a mutual friend who could present him. Otherwise, he had to find an ingenious way to make her acquaintance. He could try strolling along the same street every day at an hour when she might be walking, or attend church services where she worshipped, hoping in due time to be noticed. When all else failed, he just had to be patient and hope that an opportune circumstance would come along.

Whether on the frontier, or in a more populated area, no young girl was supposed to be with a young man without her mother's knowledge, and she *never* was to go anywhere alone with a young man in the evening. At church socials and other acceptable gatherings of young people, however, it was perfectly proper to flirt, and there were some creative ways to do this.

A young man could offer to walk a young woman home by presenting her with a card that asked if he could be her escort. She could weigh her offers and then present her own card to the one she liked the best. It was a charming gesture, well within the protocol of acceptable behavior. At more formal occasions, she could flirt with her fan. Each position had a significance of its own.

> Fan fast—I am independent
> Fan slow—I am engaged
> Fan with right hand in front of face—Come on
> Fan with left hand in front of face—Leave me
> Fan open and shut—Kiss me
> Fan open wide—Love
> Fan half open—Friendship
> Fan shut—Hate
> Fan swinging—Can I see you home?
> The *Young Ladies' Journal*, 1872

If all of this flirting succeeded in attracting the right young man, he had to demonstrate that he knew the proper rules of behavior. No well-bred, high-minded man ever ignored the carefully formulated and wisely enacted social laws.

In escorting a young lady home, he was to go up the steps with her, wait until the door was opened, and as she entered the house, raise his hat and say good night.

A-LA-MODE.

Fair One,
'Tis balmy eve, and gentle zephers blow
With mildness never known before—
Will you—kind Miss allow me to go
With you to your father's door?

R. S. V. P.
May I. C. U. Home.

COMPLIMENTS.
May 👁 C U
If not,
Please return this card.

THE ANSWER.
You cannot blame a lass like me
For thinking you quite bold;—
But if I now should answer-nay,
You'll say my heart is cold!
Kind sir, I will not judge you wrong,—
Your motives may be right;
Thus I will close by saying:
You may see me home to-night.

At formal occasions, it was quite proper for a young lady to flirt with her fan. Each position communicated a different message.

If a gentleman wished to call on a young lady at home, he was to ask permission. She, in turn, was not to receive him unless she was attended by an elder. When he did call, a gentleman was expected to carry his hat with him into the drawing room, but never to put it on a table or a chair. A well-bred man was supposed to know how to hold a hat gracefully. When saying good night, the girl was not to go any farther than the parlor door. One of the servants would show him out.

Trifling with a man's feelings, or a lady's for that matter, was not considered proper. Neither had the right to lead the other on if marriage was not their intent. And, although the young lady might be trying to catch a husband, convention did not permit her to declare her love. He must do that first.

Both were encouraged to become thoroughly acquainted before they considered marriage. A lady who would accept a gentleman at first sight could not possibly possess the discretion necessary to be a good wife, according to *Decorum* of 1886. The qualifications that did make a good wife were given in an old "receipt" that *Godey's Lady's Book* printed in 1872.

> As much of beauty as preserves affection,
> Of modest diffidence as claims protection;
> A docile mind, subservient to correction,
> A temper led by reason and reflection,
> And every passion kept in due subjection;
> Just faults enough to keep her from perfection—
> Find this, my friend, and then make your selection.

The Proposal

The many books on behavior were not very helpful when it came to giving a young man advice on how to propose.

He had to decide for himself. Although it took some courage, the gentleman was advised to propose in person so as to receive the answer from the girl's own lips. His declaration was to be bold, manly, and earnest, so that there could be no misunderstanding on her part as to his intentions. If he didn't have the courage to do this in person, then he could resort to making his proposal in writing.

Custom ruled that the lady could be coy. She did not have to accept the first time he proposed. She was to be allowed time to make up her mind. But if he should persist, courtesy decreed that she accept or regret, and if the answer was "no," to be kind and dignified about it. The rejected suitor had a duty to accept the lady's decision and to retire from the field. Etiquette rules denied him the right to demand any explanation of her refusal.

Contrary to popular perception, the young man did not ask her father for the young woman's hand in marriage before the proposal. Rather, he proposed to her first, and then, after she accepted, he went to her parents for approval, mentioning his state of affection for their daughter and giving an account of his resources and general prospects. If he was not well known to them, it was their responsibility to investigate his reputation and his character before they sanctioned the engagement.

Once her parents approved, the mother of the young man was then expected to call on his betrothed and at the same time to inquire about her mother. This visit was to be returned by both mother and daughter in ten days. If his family lived at a distance, then a letter from them to her father and mother was in order. A friendly note to the young lady welcoming her to the family was also in order. The proper procedure was for the letter to be sent to her in care of her father. Sometimes, when the families of the betrothed couple were friends or acquaintances of many years, the gentleman's side sent a friendly note of welcome with a box of flowers, or they might make a present of some family treasure to the young lady.

After this, if distance allowed, the girl's family invited the man's immediate family to a dinner to exchange felicitations and to decide when and how the engagement would be announced. The gentleman's family reciprocated with a dinner of their own.

Thus, the engagement became a reality.

The Engagement

The betrothal period was a happy time, full of activity.

Announcing the News

The first event was the announcement. It wasn't a matter of who would make it—that prerogative belonged to the bride's family. It was how. It could be a quiet affair with only intimate friends of the family present, or a grand party arranged to celebrate the engagement.

Usually, at a private dinner, the good news was not announced until after the dessert was removed, although the guests surmised the reason for the dinner when they observed the engaged daughter seated at the right hand of her father at the table, and the mother escorted into dinner by the young man. When the wine was served, the father lifted his glass and drank to the health of his future son-in-law, mentioning the name of his daughter's betrothed. Everyone at the table responded by lifting their wine glasses, and bowing to the young man. He, in turn, thanked the host and the guests, bowed first to her father, then her mother, then his betrothed and finally to the guests at the table and drank to their happiness. They, in turn, lifted their glasses and bowed back to him. Everyone wished the couple happiness and good fortune.

In addition to the formal announcement made by the bride's family, it was quite appropriate, and, in fact, highly desirable for the young man and young lady to write short notes to their closest friends, or to pay calls of intention, to make their engagement known. This form of communication was considered the most intimate. The rest was left up to "the wings of the air," since good-natured gossip could be relied upon to spread the word. The most refined and best-bred people never announced an engagement through the newspapers.

The gentleman's friends usually gave him a dinner to congratulate him after he had announced his engagement, and each one of his intimate friends then requested permission to call on the young lady.

The Engagement Ring

The betrothal was officially confirmed with a ring that was to be worn by the young lady on the ring finger of her left hand. The beauty and size of the ring depended on the groom's finances as well as the fashion of the time. Stones could be set in gold decorated with black enamel, in gold love knots symbolic of eternal love, as a solitaire, or diagonally in combination with another stone. It was customary for the gentleman to ask the young lady to express her preference. In responding, she was to be prudent in considering his finances. Sentiment had no

Engagement rings varied in style depending on the finances of the gentleman, the preferences of the young lady, and the fashions of the time. Three popular styles were the gold love knot set with a diamond, since the knot with no beginning or end was symbolic of eternal love; diamonds combined with other gems such as rubies or sapphires; and the marquise that was so popular in the late Victorian era.

A cluster ring of diamonds and sapphires. If the bride preferred, it could be set with diamonds and rubies.

Diamond marquise ring.

The love-knot ring with one diamond in the center.

small role in the final decision. A diamond was the supreme choice, for it signified innocence; a sapphire symbolized immortal life; a ruby, warm affection; an emerald, success in love. If either one of the couple was superstitious, they did not choose a pearl, for a German superstition of the time believed that pearls meant tears for the bride. A similar superstition prevailed about opals and emeralds, although this was not necessarily accepted by everyone.

When the Prince of Wales, Albert Edward, became engaged to Princess Alexandra of Denmark in 1862, he gave her a ring set with stones that spelled out his pet name, "Bertie."

The stones set in order were:

B — Beryl
E — Emerald
R — Ruby
T — Turquoise
I — Iacynth
E — Emerald

A diamond was added to represent Alexandra, since another name for that stone was Adamis.

This ring, which was a broad band with the stones set in a circle around it, was known as a gypsy ring. Jewelry that spelled out a word was not new, but its revival by royalty made it an important fashion. Some of the words most frequently used were "Amour," "Regard," and "Amité."

Some Victorians preferred to have the gypsy ring set with just diamonds, sapphires, etc., rather than with those that spelled out a name or a word. In this way, they could emulate royalty while avoiding the stones that were associated with superstitions. Besides, some believed that using one type of jewel made a handsomer ring.

Although it was not required, it was both proper and customary for the lady to give an engagement ring to the gentleman. He was to wear it on the third finger of his left hand or on the little finger. Inside the rings, the date of the engagement and the initials of each were engraved. Queen Victoria gave such a ring to her "dearest Albert" that was engraved with the date on which she proposed

Once engaged, it was quite proper for a young man to give small gifts to his fiancée, provided they were not too personal or too extravagant. A romantic card in the form of a fan embellished with delicate flowers and love poems could speak quite eloquently of his love without overstepping the bounds of etiquette. (Photograph by Scott Bowron)

to him: October 15, 1839. He gave her a serpent ring, a symbol of longevity.

Besides the engagement ring, the etiquette permitted a gentleman to offer other small presents to his bride-to-be from time to time while they were engaged, as long as they were not too personal. If she didn't think this was appropriate, he could send flowers instead. Romantic cards were always appropriate.

Choosing the Attendants

One of the first things that every prospective bride and groom needed to do after the exchange of engagement rings was to select the attendants for their wedding. She chose the bridesmaids, the ushers, and the maid of honor, or lady of honor as she was sometimes called, and he chose the best man and the groomsmen. The number of attendants varied over the decades, but their role in the wedding was to make the marriage of the young couple an occasion for happiness.

The attendants could be invited by word of mouth, or more formally by letter. Dick's *Letter Writer for Ladies* published in 1884 offered a model letter for such an invitation.

Letter from a Bride-Elect to a friend Inviting Her to be a Bridesmaid

> 4 Portland Place, Dec. 3d, 18 –.
>
> Dear Fannie:
>
> Do you remember our compact to stand bridesmaid for each other when the services of that maiden were first required? I write to claim the fulfillment of that promise.
>
> My engagement to Mr. Frederick Clay will not, I think, surprise you, as you have so often noticed his ardent attentions, and, I think, suspected that I was not indifferent to him. We have been friends too long for me to entirely hide from you the affections his many good qualities excited in my heart, and I may now throw aside all reserve and tell you I love him as I believe he loves me.
>
> We have not yet decided upon the day for our wedding, but it will be early in the New Year, so hold yourself in readiness to keep your long standing promise.
>
> With much love, dear Fannie.
>
> Yours,
>
> Josie D. Lee

Traditionally, all the members of the bridal party were to be unmarried, and ideally they would be relatives, such as brothers or sisters, or the most intimate of friends. *Decorum* in 1886 went so far as to state that the bridesmaids should be younger than the bride.

Proper Behavior for an Engaged Couple

Long engagements were not encouraged, lest the lovers find imperfections in one another. Three months from the day of the announcement to the day of the wedding was considered appropriate. This interval was filled with dinner parties, theater parties, and supper parties given by friends to introduce the young couple to a wider social circle. It was a time of enchantment for both of them. Although there were no showers per se, girl friends of the bride also gave luncheons for her where she was presented with gifts that would help her start housekeeping.

During the engagement period, the behavior of the young man and young lady was expected to be above reproach. The gentleman was in a most delicate position. Not yet a member of her family, he was to be interested and devoted, but could not assume to be too familiar. His position was that of a petitioner, and he had to be on his good behavior at all times. This meant that he had to be thoughtful in making his calls. A two-hour visit to her at her home was considered quite adequate and was not to go beyond ten o'clock in the evening.

An engaged lady was advised to be extremely guarded in her manners toward other men. She was not to correspond with them, nor permit any attentions from them. Above all, she was not to flirt with other men and her fiancé was not to display jealousy.

They were not to be overly demonstrative in public. However, as an engaged couple, they could take arms as they walked in the street; they could go to church together; they could show their preference for one another, provided they were delicate about it. A gentleman could escort his fiancée on a short journey, if her maid accompanied her, and they could go out for a drive in the carriage as long as a maid sat in the back. In New York, where society liked to emulate European standards, engaged couples were expected to be chaperoned, even if they went to Delmonico's for lunch.

It was quite proper, too, for her to visit his family if they lived at some distance, provided he had a mother and sisters. A young lady could not visit her future father-in-law at his home unless there were ladies present.

Naming the Day

According to social custom, the gentleman asked the lady to name the wedding day. This was her prerogative. He could do so in person, or by letter, and she could respond in kind.

If she chose to respond in writing, the *Ladies' Hand-Book of Letter Writing* of 1851 suggested this form.

My dear Sir,

The affectionate letter which I have just received is another convincing proof of your attachment. Upon perusing it, I find that you have imposed upon me the duty, to which, as you may conclude, I feel no aversion. You wish me to name some day, convenient to myself, as well as my relatives, for the due performance of our nuptial ceremony. You appear to be anxious that the day, to which we have looked forward as the most propitious of our future life, may not be protracted to a distant period. As far as my own choice is concerned, you may rest assured that I shall not interpose the least delay; but I have relatives and friends, by whose convenience I must, as you are aware, be in some measure restrained. I will consult them, however, without loss of time, and by an early opportunity you shall hear the decision to which we have come, either in a letter from a member of my family, or in one from,

My dear sir,

Yours most affectionately,

"_____."

Although some Victorians waited until the gentleman could afford to support a household before they named the day, most chose a day within the customary time frame of three months. Religious and family considerations influenced the decision. So, too, did superstition. There were lucky days and lucky months, days to be avoided, and one month, May, not to be considered at all, because according to an ancient prejudice that the Victorians chose not to challenge: "Marry in May and rue the day."

Monday, Tuesday, and Wednesday were all believed to be good days.

Monday for wealth
Tuesday for health
Wednesday, the best day of all.

Thursday had no major problems, but Friday was to be avoided because it was considered an evil day to start anything important, and Saturday was the most unlucky day of all. Sunday, being the Sabbath, was out of the question. So, too, was Lent: "Marry in Lent, you'll live to repent."

As for the month, June was thought to be the luckiest. According to the *Ladies' Home Journal* of June 1891, "Whoever is married during its long sunshiny days will not only be happy all her life, but will always retain the love of her husband." If the wedding was to be in the fall, October was an auspicious month.

For Victorians living in rural areas, especially in the early years, weddings were planned for March, April, November, or December so as not to conflict with the months when farm work would be at a peak. In the South, an April wedding immediately after Easter was favored partly because their favorite flowers—jasmine and camellia—were in bloom, but mostly because the weather later on would be too hot.

Once the day had been named, the next decision was the time and the place.

In the East, the most fashionable hour for a wedding was noon or sometime between ten o'clock and noon, because this was the English custom. In New York in 1890, half after three o'clock in the afternoon was also a favorite hour. Not all weddings were held during the day. Some Victorians chose to have an evening wedding, especially if the marriage ceremony was to be at home. Southern weddings, on the other hand, were almost always held at six o'clock in the evening because it was cooler then.

The decision as to whether the wedding would be in a church or at home was partly influenced by religion and partly by custom. During the 1850s New York Episcopalian society was beginning to look down on weddings held at home. They were considered to be the last resort for religious sects with no altars. However, some still felt

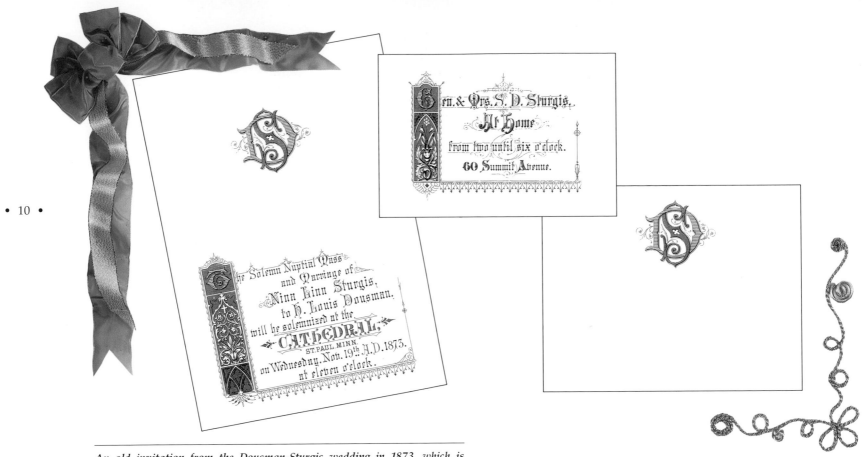

An old invitation from the Dousman-Sturgis wedding in 1873, which is somewhat worn in one corner, with a monogram of the two initials on the envelope. The At Home card was for the wedding breakfast. Although the social arbiters of New York insisted that script was the only correct lettering for invitations, all Victorians did not necessarily agree, as can be seen in this example. (Courtesy Villa Louis Historic Site, Prairie du Chien, Wisconsin)

that a marriage at home offered greater privacy and that this made up for the impersonal atmosphere of a church. By 1890, at-home weddings were back in favor.

Inviting the Guests

If the wedding was to be held at a church, no matter how small, social custom dictated that invitations must be engraved. The only acceptable lettering was script. Neither Old English nor German Text was admissible. For a small wedding at home—fifty or fewer guests—the invitations could be written by hand on note paper decorated with a monogram or a family crest.

The most admired form for the invitation was as follows:

Mr. and Mrs. Howard Mortimer
request your presence
at the marriage of their daughter,
Matilde Alice,
to
Mr. Alexis Stafford Carlton,
on Tuesday morning, October tenth,
at eleven o'clock.
St. John's Cathedral,
New York.

An invitation to the wedding breakfast was enclosed in the same envelope. It was to be a square card, the same size as the invitation for the ceremony after it had been folded once across the middle.

Mr. and Mrs. Howard Mortimer
request the pleasure of

Mr. and Mrs. James Jenkyns

company at breakfast, on
Tuesday, October tenth
at half-past eleven o'clock.

321 Plaza Place.

The name of the invited guest was handwritten on the invitation.

Another form of invitation for the breakfast following a noon wedding could read:

AT HOME
Tuesday, October tenth
from 12 until 3 o'clock.
321 Plaza Place.

In addition, there was a third smaller card for admission to the church. This was long and narrow and engraved in the same script as the invitation.

Please present this card at
St. John's Cathedral
October tenth.

When a bride had a stepfather, the wedding invitation was to be worded:

Mr. and Mrs. John Monroe
request the honor of your presence
at the marriage of their daughter
Mary Louise Smith

(Smith being the bride's own last name).

By mentioning the bride's own last name, there could be no misunderstanding on the part of those who received the invitation, and, at the same time, the stepfather was not slighted. It would have been considered bad form for the invitations to be extended by the bride's mother alone, especially if the stepfather had been married to her for a long time.

Whatever the form, it was considered poor taste to state "No Presents Received" on the invitation. Dates were usually written out. Figures were considered vulgar by some social leaders, and no year was indicated because it was obvious.

The etiquette of the wedding invitation was subtle but significant. For a church wedding, the wording stated, "the honor of your presence is requested," whereas, at home, it was "the pleasure of your company is desired." A church wedding was formal, the role of the guest passive. At home, social intercourse was implied.

Early in the Victorian era, it was customary to have square invitations; later, in the 1890s, the preference was for an invitation measuring 6" x 8", which could be folded once to fit into an envelope. The most fashionable style in 1898 was a 6½" x 5" invitation, folded once to fit into a 5½" x 3" envelope. All were to be on thick paper of a fine quality.

Invitations were sent fifteen days before the wedding by private messenger in the mid-Victorian years because to send them by post was considered to be in poor taste, and by post in the later years because the Victorians didn't trust servants to deliver them without losing some.

It was not customary to respond to an invitation. Etiquette made it perfectly clear that anyone invited to the wedding was expected to attend unless something very extraordinary should happen. The proper form was to send one's calling card on the day of the wedding. If one also received an invitation to the wedding breakfast, then an answer was in order.

Brides in the South followed a tradition unique to that region. Wedding invitations were printed on wide bands of satin ribbon that had been fringed at both ends and mounted on a longer piece of parchment, which was folded over to form a protective envelope. These were delivered by family servants.

Sending Announcements

Announcement cards for a wedding were sent immediately after the wedding to those not invited to the marriage ceremony. Sometimes these cards were highly ornamented, or at the minimum had borders of silver. They were, of course, engraved. A marriage announcement did not demand an acknowledgment.

The proper wording for an announcement was:

Mr. and Mrs. Seth Osborne
announce the marriage of their daughter
Marguerite
to
Mr. Joseph Wendon,
on
Wednesday, September the ninth,
at
Bristol, Connecticut,
At Home after January first,
at 758 Wood Street.

The announcement for a widow who remarried usually read:

Married
on the twentieth of September
eighteen hundred and ninety-eight
at St. Mary's Church
Detroit
Mary Louise Parker
to
William Blake.

Her name included her late husband's surname as well as her Christian name.

Sometimes the announcement card had enclosed with it an "At Home" card mentioning the time and the hours the newly married couple would be "at home" to receive guests. An earlier custom of enclosing both the groom's card and the bride's card was dropped in the late 1890s. For those who attended the wedding, cards were sent out two weeks before the first "At Home" day.

It was generally recognized and accepted that there were limitations to the hospitality that a young couple could extend so that no one was offended if they did not receive a card. The omission was the signal that one was no longer on the social list of the newly married pair.

While all this activity was taking place, the bride-to-be and her mother were assembling her trousseau and arranging details of the wedding. *Harper's Bazar* of November 8, 1890 stated that a month was long enough to make these plans.

The Bride's Trousseau

The bride's trousseau was something every girl talked and dreamed about long before she was old enough to be a bride. It included her wedding dress, a wardrobe of new gowns, at least a year's supply of delicate undergarments trimmed with tucks, laces, and embroidery, and all her household linens for ten years. Even the paper dolls in magazines such as *Godey's Lady's Book* had a trousseau.

A bride-to-be and her friends spent hours discussing what she should have in her trousseau and, when it was all assembled, they spent more hours admiring it.

The wedding dress was, of course, the most romantic piece in the trousseau, and probably even the most expensive. Generally speaking, brides from the East looked to the fashion trends from Paris in selecting the silhouette and the color for the dress of their dreams, while brides in the West looked to the big cities in the East.

The Early Victorian Wedding Dress

In the early Victorian era wedding dresses reflected the stereotype of the fragile female. The bodice (or corsage as it was known) was fitted, the waist was small and the skirt was very full, supported by many petticoats of crinoline and horsehair. They were made of such delicate-looking fabrics as organdy, tulle, lace, gauze, silk, linen, and cashmere. The veil was a fine gauze, sheer cotton, or lace. As skirts became more bouffant (some were made from as many as twenty-five yards of fabric) the gentle sway of a full skirt supported by a hoop cage merely added to the feminine impression of the bride walking down the aisle.

Empress Eugénie of France, who married Louis Napoleon III on January 3, 1853 had a tremendous influence on fashion at this time. Her wedding dress for

A bridal dress similar to the one worn by Empress Eugénie of France in 1853. The bride is wearing white lilacs in her hair. (Harper's New Monthly Magazine)

the religious ceremony was of lace and satin with a wide skirt. *Harper's New Monthly Magazine* featured a bridal dress fashioned after the one worn by Eugénie. The description is quite detailed, one that could have been used by a bride in America to create her own adaptation of this fashion.

We present a Bridal Dress very similar to that worn by the Empress of France. Dress of terry velvet, ornamented with passementerie and lace. The body high, and very close, is prolonged down to the hips. It is trimmed in front with buttons and guipure, and ears of satin passementerie laid in chevrons. These ears, graduated, are 2½ inches at top, 1½ toward the waist, and rather over three inches at bottom. A narrow engrelure borders the bottom of the body, which is terminated by a lace of 6 inches, slightly gathered. The skirt has beautiful lace flounces. A lace collar, gathered, falls over the body. But a frill of tulle illusion ruché goes round the neck. The sleeves, of pagoda form, are trimmed with three rows of lace, looped up to a button and sewed under a little passementerie engrelure. The two first rows are on the sleeve; the third is sewed to the edge, and falls very full, like an undersleeve.

*A fashion plate in the December 1861 issue of **Godey's Lady's Book** featured a lace wedding dress (see figure at left) that could not be imported for under one thousand or fifteen hundred dollars. The price depended on the fineness of the lace.*

GODEY'S FASHIONS FOR DECEMBER 1861.

Since the arrangement of the hair was an integral part of the bridal toilette, the magazine also gave detailed instructions for how to achieve the look that was illustrated.

The hair is arranged in puffed bandeaux rolled one above another, and very finely undulated. A narrow bandeau of white lilac passes over the head, and is lost in each extremity between the origin of the bandeaux of hair. Two tufts of double hyacinths and branches of white lilac inclose the bandeaux behind, and accompany them below. A crown of orange-flowers is laid behind, over the comb. The veil of tulle illusion is thrown back so as to cover the crown and the top of the tufts of flowers; this veil is very large.

This was a time when more families in America were beginning to accumulate wealth and spending rather extravagantly for the bride's trousseau was not uncommon. In 1850, *Godey's Lady's Book* stated that $500 was "reasonable indeed, my dears, for a wedding dress, and for the veil $125."

By 1861, in the December fashion plate, *Godey's* featured one wedding dress "which could not be imported under a thousand or fifteen hundred dollars (according to the fineness of the lace)."

It was described as an extremely rich lace robe over white silk with a combination of Brussels and point Duchess lace, the graceful design having a border of medallions, and the same pattern of medallions being repeated at the height of the knee. The sleeves and body were of white silk; the corsage was high, with a pointed bertha of lace in the same pattern as the border of the robe, but narrower; a double row of the same lace was used on the long flowing sleeves, which were caught up by a knot of silver fringe. The veil of Brussels lace exactly matched that used on the gown.

A few years later in January 1867, *Godey's* featured another imported dress, not quite so extravagant, but still one that would have cost an indulgent Victorian father a handsome sum. The dress was of heavy white satin with a very long train. The skirt was gored, appliquéd with rich lace to resemble a tunic, and decorated with rosettes of lace. The corsage was high and perfectly plain—a French touch meant to convey modesty and delicacy on the part of the bride. The long plain sleeves and the small collar were trimmed with lace.

Such extravagances were really not as outrageous as they might seem, inasmuch as the bride's gown was worn after the wedding for balls and other formal occasions and the veil often served as a shawl.

For those who were fortunate enough to go to England to be presented to the queen, and this was the goal of many American matrons at the time, the wedding dress could also be worn for the ceremony at court. The requirements for dress at this formal occasion were a white gown of sufficient richness, correctly modest, with a veil, white shoes and stockings, and a white bouquet. Queen Victoria was particularly adamant about the white shoes and stockings.

Formal weddings during this period were usually all white, including the gowns worn by the bridesmaids, who, like the bride, wore white veils that fell to below the waist. The veil was attached to a coronet of flowers,

• 15 •

Waiting in "The Pen" for presentation to the queen.

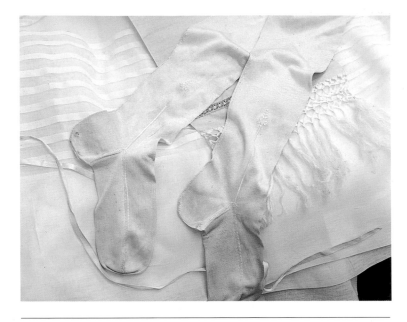

The fancy silk stockings in the collection at The Hermitage in Ho-Ho-Kus, New Jersey, were originally worn by a bride in 1848, and then by her daughter in 1872. One of the brides had darned a small hole near the top. They were too precious to be thrown away. (Photograph by G F Studio / Rob Kern)

Early Victorian bridal headdress. (Peterson's Magazine, 1858)

orange blossoms (real or waxed) for the bride, and roses or other flowers in season for the bridesmaids. It did not cover the face, but instead fell from the back of the crown.

The bride wore short white kid gloves and carried a small tight posey of flowers in one hand along with an elaborate handkerchief embroidered with the initials of her maiden name. These handkerchiefs were tucked away carefully after the wedding to be saved for the next generation of brides in the family. So, too, were the stockings. They were usually made of white silk with delicate designs knit or embroidered up the front. Her shoes were flat with bows or ribbons across the instep.

Some brides, following the example set by Empress Engénie, carried a prayer book rather than a posey.

Fashions for dressing the hair were just as important as the dress. Both the bride and her bridesmaids looked to those who shaped the trends for the latest styles in "coiffures."

The extravagant wedding dress of 1861 called for the hair to be turned back from the face and dressed low to conceal the ear.

The bride pictured in the fashion plate of 1867 (see page 33) had her hair heavily crimped and dressed with a bandeau of fine white flowers with a rich appliqué lace veil.

A selection of bridal garments from The Hermitage collection. The bridal dress is made of white lawn, c. 1870, with tiny tucks over the bodice, with a high neck and long sleeves. The cuffs and collar are trimmed with feather stitching. The sash is ecru silk-faille ribbon. The white kid boots, laced up the side, were worn by Welthy Sheets at her wedding in 1872. The veil was loaned by Ellen McClelland Lesser. (Photograph by G F Studio / Rob Kern)

The Frontier Bride

For the frontier bride in the decades of the 1850s and the 1860s, the bridal gown was quite another matter. Although a wedding was an important event, the dress worn on that special day would have to be used afterwards for churchgoing and other special occasions. Some brides wore white, but most chose a variety of colors in cambric, wool, or linen.

One colorful wedding accessory that many frontier brides brought with them was a warm shawl, usually of wool and preferably woven in a paisley or plaid design. It was draped around her shoulders at the wedding, and used later for christenings, social events, or even bedding when extra warmth was needed. A warm shawl was more cherished than a wedding dress.

Not all wedding dresses were white. The frontier bride had to be practical and often chose cambric wool or linen in a pattern that would be suitable for many occasions after the wedding. (Daguerreotype courtesy America Hurrah Antiques, N.Y.C.; photograph by Scott Bowron)

The Mid-Victorian Wedding Dress

The decade of the 1870s saw the emergence of middle-class Victorians, and with this came the emphasis on material possessions to display status. The bride's trousseau was no exception.

A wedding gown by Worth of Paris was the ultimate status symbol for a bride. Having won the patronage of the Empress Eugénie, Charles Worth had become a famous designer who influenced fashion in Europe and America. His bridal dresses were made of a lustrous white satin commissioned from the silk weavers of Lyons, France. Because he was couturier to royalty in Europe, Worth fashioned the court train for bridal dresses and was the first to use the long wedding veil. His dresses had elegant details including embroidery, jewels, ruffles, and pleated lace. Many of the gowns were made with two bodices, one with a high neck to be worn for the marriage ceremony and another, more décolleté one to be used later when the gown was worn again for special occasions. Due to Worth's influence, white became the predominant color for wedding dresses in the mid-Victorian era.

A middle-class bride might not be able to afford a Worth gown, but she could adapt some of the details to create her own. Help was available from many sources. She could send swatches of fabrics to editors at the many ladies' magazines who would then give direct advice through their "Answers to Correspondence" columns, even to the point of telling her what *not* to do.

> For your wedding dress get white heavily repped silk and orange blossoms. Make with a flowing train edged with a deep ruche, basque with pointed neck, and very slight panier drapery. Do not *combine* materials in a new dress.
>
> *Harper's Bazar,* 1882

These publications were one of the principal windows on the world of society both in Europe and America, which middle-class ladies could look to for the definitive word on fashion news for each season. Not only did they illustrate the new styles but they also published a supplement with patterns and specific directions.

beaded tulle over plain satin that was held at the bottom of the dress by a wide satin scarf fastened with a bow and a buckle of brilliants. This scarf headed a wide piece of lace decorated with orange blossoms, and below it were six rows of narrow lace. The wide lace and orange blossoms were also arranged down each side of the skirt.

The front of the bodice, or basque as it was called, was pointed at the neckline, finely pleated and trimmed with lace and orange blossoms. The lower part was rounded and caught in pleats. This was topped with a ribbon and bow at the waist with a buckle of brilliants, just like the one on the skirt. The elbow sleeves had a tiny cuff, trimmed with flowers and lace. On her corsage (bodice) she wore a bouquet (or corsage, as it was called later) of orange blossoms.

The long veil was unhemmed tulle, her gloves were white undressed kid, and she carried an ivory-bound prayer book.

An elegant Parisian bridal toilette of white satin damask. The bride is wearing a corsage bouquet. (Harper's Bazar, September 30, 1882)

They described in detail many of the fashionable weddings of the day so that young ladies could pattern their own weddings after the customs set by those in society.

The bride's gown of this era was very elaborate. The wide hooped skirt had gradually changed to a skirt with all the fullness formed into a bustle in the back. Instead of a crinoline, she wore a foundation skirt with three dress steels in casings across the back. Rich details, such as scallops, tiny pleats, flounces, and braiding were used lavishly, due in part, no doubt, to the influence of Worth.

The mid-Victorian bride of the 1870s and 1880s had a wedding coat as well as a gown. This was the same length as the dress and was lined with material to match. White satin or kid boots, buttoned up the side, completed her toilette.

A dress representative of all this elegance was featured in the September 30, 1882 issue of *Harper's Bazar*. It was described as a Parisian toilette for a bride composed of white satin damask, plain satin, and tulle dotted with pearl beads. The square train was trimmed up the sides and across the end with a very heavy ruche (pleated strip) of lace. The tablier (front panel) was

manner of dressing the hair without the veil is shown in Fig. 4. The veil is of silk tulle, three yards wide and three yards and a quarter long; the lower corners are rounded, and the edge is hemmed two inches and a half wide all around. The top is clearly pleated into a small space at three inches from the upper edge, and tied with a narrow silk ribbon; the heading above the tying is then spread apart to form a large full rosette, which is fastened on the crown, partly covering the wreath; the latter, which is of orange leaves and blossoms, is thick and full at the front, and tapers at the sides. The folds of the veil are pinned to the hair with fine invisible hairpins.

"To arrange the hair as shown in Fig. 4, it is first parted from side to side, after which the back hair is divided horizontally, and the upper portion is tied. The front hair is parted at the middle, and the lower part on each side is brought back and pinned to the tied back hair. The lower back hair is then divided into two, puffed slightly, and brought up on each side, while the upper part of the front hair is waved and brought back to hang in two curls behind. The tied portion of the back hair is twisted into a knot on the crown, which is fastened with shell pins. The short front locks are curled lightly to fall on the forehead.

"The point lace veil draped in Fig. 2 is four yards long and twenty-four inches wide. The middle is pleated up and secured to the hair with a spray of orange blossoms and white rosebuds, while on the sides the veil is festooned and fastened to the corsage with similar bouquets.

"The same coiffure without the veil and ornamented with square shell pins is shown in Fig. 3. The hair is parted from ear to ear, and the back hair is combed high and tied on the crown. The front hair is parted in the middle and waved, and is then brought back, the lower portion on each side first, then the upper part over it, and pinned to the back hair. The latter is then divided into three strands, each of which is puffed slightly, then twisted upon itself and pinned to the head. When the natural hair is insufficient it is coiled into a tight knot at the top of the back, and a switch attached to a narrow comb is fastened on over it, and twisted into the three coils previously described. The short hair on the forehead is curled and combed out."

As gowns became more formal, so too did the bride's coiffure. These four bridal coiffures were featured in **Harper's Bazar**, with the following description. "Fig. 1 shows the arrangement of a tulle bridal veil and wreath; the

Although white was the predominant color, it was by no means the only color chosen by mid-Victorian brides. Blue, gray, and plum were also worn for formal weddings. At a society wedding in Dubuque, Iowa, in 1874, the bride wore a gown of lavender silk trimmed with orange blossoms. Her veil was of white tulle. The Hermitage in Ho-Ho-Kus, New Jersey, has in its collection an elegant gown of gray silk taffeta, with a long train and a lace tablier.

Such regal gowns called for a coiffure that was equally grand. Here, again, the ladies' magazines printed detailed illustrations and gave directions for achieving the proper arrangement of the hair and the veil.

The Late Victorian Wedding Dress

By the 1890s, the bustle was gone, but the train or demitrain was very much in fashion. So, too, were large sleeves that emphasized the shoulder. The tiny waist continued to be important, much to the distress of some brides who fainted from the tight corset that had to be used to create the illusion of a tiny waist.

If it was to be a formal church wedding, fashion decreed that the bride's dress must have a train and that the veil must be at least as long as the dress. The veil could be lace, especially if it was an heirloom, but silk tulle was preferred. According to *Harper's Bazar* of July 26, 1890, a true wedding veil measured four square yards, meaning two yards long on each of the four sides. The veil could be plain or embroidered with silk floss, but it was not to be hemmed. The supplement for the same date printed a design for a border of myrtle that could be embroidered on a veil as well as orange-blossom designs for the wedding dress.

From the mid-Victorian years to the beginning of the 1890s, the veil covered the bride's face and was not lifted

An 1895 bridal dress from the collection at The Hermitage. It is ecru silk with a train. The dress has an attached petticoat with a deep pleated underruffle called a balayeuse. The bodice is bloused with a deep lace yolk and a high neck with an elegant collar decorated with French knots. (Photograph by G F Studio / Rob Kern)

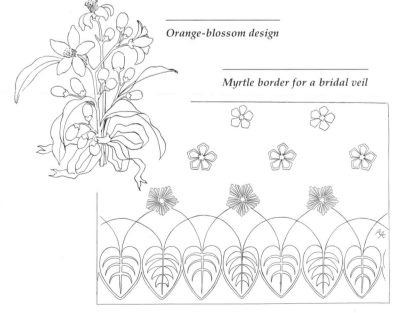

Orange-blossom design

Myrtle border for a bridal veil

A sentimental bride could embroider orange blossoms on her dress and myrtle on her veil. A lustrous white Oriental floss was recommended for such embroidery. (Harper's Bazar, July 26, 1890)

until she and her husband had left the church after the ceremony. In later years, some brides had the veil draped from the back of the head and did not cover their face. Princess May of Teck, who later became Queen Mary of England, wore her veil in this fashion. Contrary to the custom of earlier times, the veil was the only piece in the wedding toilette that was not to be worn again after the wedding.

The formal bridal toilette called for undressed white kid gloves and the traditional bride's handkerchief with an elaborately embroidered border, monogrammed with her family initials.

The length of the gloves varied. They were to be long enough to extend inside the dress sleeves and were worn loosely wrinkled at the wrist. In the early and mid-Victorian years it was customary to rip open the inner seam of the third finger of the left glove beforehand, so that the wedding ring could be slipped on the bride's finger during the marriage ceremony without necessitating removal of the glove. Later on, this practice came to be considered the "traditional" approach and brides were encouraged, instead, to remove the glove from the left hand before the ceremony.

The bride's slippers were made of white kid, satin, or brocade with one-inch heels. They could be plain or decorated with a rosette of fabric centered with orange blossoms. Her white stockings, knit of pure silk like those in earlier decades, could have fancy clockwork up the side, be embroidered with orange blossoms in white floss up the front, or appliquéd with lace medallions, depending on which style was most appropriate with her dress. These were displayed with her trousseau before the wedding, and afterward they were laid away in lavender as an heirloom.

Most brides respected the old superstition that said she should wear

Something old, something new
Something borrowed, something blue.

To ensure the good luck of this belief, the something borrowed had to be a thing of real value that she truly intended to return, not just a sentimental souvenir of some member of the family. The something blue could be a garter she might have received as a bridesmaid at a friend's wedding. Brides often gave these to their unmarried bridesmaids. They were blue, with a gold buckle engraved, not with the bridesmaid's initials, but with those of the bride.

A wedding gown from Paris was still the ultimate status symbol in the 1890s, but if this wasn't possible, a dress made in the French fashion, reflecting the newest trends of the season, was quite acceptable.

Harper's Bazar of 1898 pictured one of the newest styles in a wedding gown. It was white satin with a very long plain front that was caught up at each side with a rosette of white tulle. The long train was entirely covered with lace, very wide at the bottom, and narrower at the top to avoid unnecessary fullness at the waist. The bodice was tight, plain in the back, draped in the front in soft folds that were fastened at the bust with a large tulle rosette. It had a narrow pleated tulle vest and a bolero of white lace on the upper part. The sleeves were full at the top, but tight fitting as they went down the arm. They came to a point over the hand finished with a chiffon "plisse." A long spray of orange blossoms fell down the front of the skirt.

The headdress was of white tulle and orange blossoms, and the tulle veil, in a fashion which was popular in the late Victorian era, fell from the back.

Not all bridal fashions were this elaborate. The *Ladies'*

A handkerchief lavishly edged with lace was an important accessory for the bridal toilette that was passed on from generation to generation.

A new French fashion for a bridal gown. (Harper's Bazar, October 8, 1898)

• 21 •

Ostrich feathers trim the train of this late Victorian dress. (Harper's Bazar, September 26, 1891)

A sumptuous bridal toilette in white grosgrain silk and white chiffon with a long train. A fan of chiffon headed with a bunch of orange blossoms is inserted at each knee. The bouqet is lilies of the valley and foliage. (The Delineator, June 1896)

Home Journal in June 1891 featured what they considered a simple fashion made of white cloth with white figures embossed on it. The dress had a full train of plain white cloth. A deep frill of old lace, which they suggested might have been worn by the bride's mother, was attached to the pointed waist of the basque. To give the gown a long-waisted appearance, there was a V-shaped motif of white pearl in the front. The gown had a high rolled collar, overlaid with pearl passementerie. The full sleeves had "vandyke" cutouts with puffs of flowered fabric showing through. The veil of tulle was fastened to a headdress of orange blossoms.

The Dress for the Widow Who Remarried

For the widow who wished to remarry, the early and mid-Victorians had strict guidelines. She could not wear white, she could not have bridesmaids, nor could she wear a veil and orange blossoms. These were all symbols of purity associated with unmarried ladies. She could, however, wear pearl or lavender satin trimmed with ostrich feathers and an aigrette of ostrich tips with a diamond ornament in her hair.

By the later decades of the Victorian era, however, these rules were relaxed. *Good Form Weddings*, Formal and Informal, published in 1891, had this to say about the marriage of widows:

> There was once a stateliness, if not a severity in the formalities attending marriages of widows, as if in rebuke to them for wedding again, but all that, very properly, has fallen into disuse ... Etiquette allows a widow as many bridesmaids, maids of honor, and pages as she chooses to invite, also all the sumptuousness of spectacular accessories, if she prefers such pomps. Custom, that always inflexible mistress of social affairs, denies her a veil and orange blossoms, but she wears a robe of white, if it is becoming to her, and her age does not make its appearance incongruous.
>
> As a rule, however, she chooses a shade or two away from white, preferring rose, salmon, violet, or ivory, not for any poetic reason, but because such a change is an advantage to her own color.
>
> Of course, a woman who is clever in grades of attire, and familiar with social fitness and the best of standards of

A bridal gown and a toque of pale lavender for a widow who remarried. This same costume was also appropriate for a going-away outfit. (**Ladies' Home Journal,** *June 1891*)

> taste cannot possibly make her appearance whimsical, at her marriage. A pretense of youth, after youth has taken leave of a woman, simply intensifies personal evidence of age, and is a pathetic spectacle. This is less often noticeable in a woman's dress, however, than in her manners.
>
> Fashion which is social law, no longer disapproves of rich attire, white raiment, jewels and flowers for the advanced matron, whether she is bride, wife or widow, unless she is unmistakably aged.

The *Ladies' Home Journal* of June 1891 had a gown

A bride's going-away outfit of cloth with a velvet collar. The scallops on the border of the skirt are outlined with soutache braid. (**The Delineator,** June 1896)

white undressed kid. Other suggested colors were gray cloth, tan, or wood.

The Traveling Dress

All brides did not choose to be married in a formal gown. A traveling dress was equally proper, especially if the wedding was to be an intimate affair with family and a few close friends in attendance, or if the bridal couple were going to leave immediately after the marriage ceremony for a journey by train or by steamer. Since this was a garment that would be worn often after the wedding, the colors were chosen to be both becoming and practical. Dark brown and even black were popular in the mid-Victorian era because they were considered smart.

Although it was not required, especially if the marriage ceremony was to be performed at home, most brides preferred to wear a bonnet trimmed with bows and strings to match the color of the dress.

suitable for a widow, or a going-away costume for a bride. It was a very light lavender broadcloth, so light as to give almost the impression of being gray. The front had a tablier that was wrinkled a little at each side near the top and just in the center at the foot it was slashed with a plaiting of heavy silk of the same shade visible from underneath. A braiding of silver outlined the edge.

The bodice was laced in the back, slashed and pointed about the bottom edge, and decorated with a fine braid. The upper part of the bodice was cut out in a point which was also decorated in braid. The high collar was rounded in the front and overlaid with silver braid. The same braid was used to decorate the full cap of each sleeve, as were the cuffs at the wrist. Her hat was a fancy straw one decorated with lavender flowers, and the gloves were

Traveling dress for an early Victorian bride.

• 24 •

Traveling dress for a mid-Victorian bride.

Traveling dress for a late-Victorian bride.

The bridesmaid at this type of wedding wore a visiting gown or a street dress and a bonnet. Both wore gloves.

Even though her gown was not formal, the bride carried a bouquet, in a style that was fashionable at the time.

Not all weddings in which the bride wore a traveling dress were informal. In 1892, in Princeton, Kentucky, when Mayme Smith married Mr. R. D. Garrett at a 4:30 P.M. service in the First Presbyterian Church, there were several hundred guests present. She wore a traveling dress of tan and green cloth trimmed in green velvet with gloves to match, and carried a handsome bouquet of chrysanthemums. There were no bridesmaids. The couple left on a six o'clock train for a wedding trip to Chicago.

The Bride's Jewelry

Although the jewelry worn by Victorian brides was not technically a part of the trousseau, it was an important accessory.

Diamonds were especially coveted throughout the period, and when white became the dominant color for wedding dresses, white jewelry in the form of pearls with diamonds became fashionable.

The early-Victorian bride liked matched sets of jewelry, especially diamonds. This was no doubt due in part to the influence of the Empress Eugénie who wore diamond earrings, a diamond and pearl bracelet, and a diamond belt as part of her bridal toilette.

The mid-Victorian bride was more extravagant with her jewelry, partly because she was living at a time when material possessions were an important status symbol. If the family owned a diamond tiara, she wore it for the first time on her wedding day. Princess Louise of Prussia, who married the Duke of Connaught in 1879, fastened her veil with five diamond stars, a gift from the bridegroom. This may have led to the fashion for diamond stars and diamond sunbursts being used for bridal jewelry, and especially for diamonds to be worn to hold the veil in place. Combination pieces of diamond jewelry that could be separated to become several individual pieces to be worn later on ballgowns were another innovation that Victorian brides particularly liked.

THE BRIDE'S TROUSSEAU

Breakfast cap

Lady's combing sacque

Lady's corset cover

Chemise with crochet yoke and sleeves

Muslin kitchen apron

Petticoats

Lace edging

Lady's drawers

The bride at an 1892 wedding in Brooklyn wore a diamond necklace that was the gift of the groom, while another in 1891 wore a diamond tiara, also a gift of the groom. At the Lawler-Sturgis wedding of 1886 in Prairie du Chien, Wisconsin, the bride wore a pendant of diamonds from the groom, and a magnificent pair of solitaire diamond earrings that was the present of her sister.

Traditionally, jewelry worn by the bride was a gift from the groom. Occasionally, she wore jewelry both from the groom and from her family, and if his family were especially generous, she might also wear jewelry that was a gift from them.

When a wedding was early in the day, especially at noon, the Victorian custom in the later years was for the bride's jewelry to be the gift of the groom only. An over-display of jewelry at this hour was not considered in good taste. Consuelo Vanderbilt wore no jewelry at her noon wedding to the Duke of Marlborough in 1895.

The Bride's Personal Trousseau

Although the bridal gown was the most romantic piece in her trousseau, the Victorian bride and her friends were equally concerned with all the other finery that she was to take with her to her new life.

At least four basic costumes were deemed necessary: a traveling dress, preferably of cashmere that she probably wore as her going-away outfit, a velvet costume for returning visits, an ottoman silk and brocade outfit, one or two smart gowns for house wear, and dozens of handkerchiefs. These were to be complemented with bonnets, gloves, stockings, and boots.

What created the most discussion and admiration among the bridesmaids and the bride was her trousseau of undergarments. Every young lady dreamed of the elegant finery she would like to take to her new life, and many an extravagant Victorian father indulged her wishes as he became caught up in the nostalgia of giving his daughter away. The basic articles she needed, in the order in which they would be worn, were a ribbed-silk or wool vest, drawers of cambric, linen, or percale with a yoke and a drawstring, a corset, a corset cover with sleeves and one without, a chemise and a walking-length petticoat of silk, muslin, or mohair. For cold weather she also needed ribbed, fitted wool or silk drawers and a knitted petticoat. All were trimmed with tucks and laces, and many were embroidered with the initials of her maiden name. In addition, the basic trousseau included nightgowns and a combing jacket that was worn like a negligé. How many of each she had depended on what was customary at that time. The early Victorian bride was expected to have at least two dozen of everything, while the bride of the mid years usually had only one dozen of each.

In New England, the South, and the Midwest, the

A petticoat from the collection at The Hermitage. It is off-white cotton sheer, c. 1901, with trellis-design panels and machine-made lace with a three-leaf clover design. (Photograph by G F Studio / Rob Kern)

mid-Victorian bride participated in an old custom known as "Coming Out Bride." It gave her the opportunity to display her new trousseau on the first Sunday after the wedding. The bride and groom, dressed in their new clothes, walked slowly to church, purposely arriving just a little late, so that they could be seen by the entire congregation as they were escorted to the front pew. After the congregation sang the second hymn, the newlyweds were to rise and turn slowly, facing the members of the church so that the details of the costume from the bridal trousseau could be seen by all. If a bride had four complete new outfits, she would wear a different one on each of four successive Sundays for a "Coming Out Bride" month.

On the other hand, brides of the late Victorian era were encouraged to use common sense. The prevailing attitude was that six new pieces of every type of lingerie were quite enough. Dozens of gloves, handkerchiefs, and stockings were not necessary. As for gowns, one or two new ones were sufficient, with an additional one for street wear or traveling. Those already in her wardrobe could be freshened up and included as well. A pair of boots, a pair of low shoes, one white pair and one black pair of slippers were deemed adequate. The wise bride was advised to limit her wardrobe to the season in which she was married, so that her husband would recognize early in the new season that he had a responsibility to buy her clothing. As a final touch, she was to make some pretty sachets to throw among her belongings.

The Household Trousseau

Of equal importance to her clothing was the bride's trousseau of household linens. She was to have enough of various grades from kitchen to garret to last for ten years. Many were hemstitched and most were embroidered with her maiden initials. Those brides who chose to make the flower of their wedding their special flower for life might also embroider that motif on some of their linens. If a couple was not to have a household of their own to begin with, the bride was advised to put aside some of her money so that she could buy the linens they would need after they settled. Custom decreed that this was her responsibility.

Flowers for the Bride

Throughout the Victorian era, it was traditional for the bride to wear orange blossoms in some form, either as a coronet to hold her veil (which is what Queen Victoria did), as decoration on her dress or veil, or tucked into her bouquet as Princess May did in 1893. Sometimes these were real; often they were made of wax. It didn't matter which, so long as she had orange blossoms. Once married, custom ruled that a woman could no longer wear orange blossoms. If they had decorated her dress, they were to be replaced by roses, since the dress would become part of her wardrobe. In fact, there was a belief among the Victorians that orange blossoms should be destroyed within one month of the wedding so that evil spirits wouldn't get in. The *Ladies' Home Journal* of June 1891 advised, "All these seem little things, but they have their absolute significance, and a bright woman does not wish to show the world at large her ignorance of their symbolism."

Although prayer books were carried by some brides, and baskets of flowers or fans by others, the bouquet remained important throughout the era. It was more than a bunch of flowers held together with ribbon; it was almost a love poem. Each flower and leaf was carefully selected for the sentiment associated with it. Bridal roses signified happy love; the jasmine, which was the favorite of southern brides, spoke of amiability; violets expressed innocence; the pansy said think of me; a piece of rosemary denoted refreshment; ivy leaves represented the lasting bond of matrimony, while myrtle was the symbol of constancy in affection and duty. Queen Victoria had myrtle in her bouquet, and later it was planted, so to this day, at every royal wedding in England a piece of her myrtle is either tucked into the bride's bouquet or is added to one of the floral arrangements at the wedding breakfast. It has become a family tradition.

Regardless of the variety of flowers and leaves used, the bridal bouquet was almost always white. Even the bride married in a traveling dress at a small wedding might carry one, for it was a romantic symbol. The frontier bride, of course, didn't have as much of a choice. Her bouquet was made up of whatever flowers were in bloom at the time of her wedding.

In the early years of the Victorian era, a small round posey of mixed flowers held in a tight circle was the traditional bouquet. At times this posey was so small that the bride held it in one hand, along with an elaborately embroidered lace handkerchief. It could be encircled with paper frill or with real lace. Sometimes the posey was arranged in moss in a delicate filigree bouquet holder with a ring that slipped on the bride's finger. The posey increased somewhat in size over the years, but it remained the most popular bridal bouquet into the late Victorian era.

This is not to say that innovations in how the flowers were arranged in the posey did not occur. The bouquet at the White House wedding of Nellie Grant and Algernon C.F. Sartoris in 1874 was made up of tuberoses and orange blossoms with a small silver banner inserted in the center inscribed with the word *love*.

Gradually, especially toward the end of the era, the bridal bouquet, like many other Victorian decorations, became more elaborate. By the late 1880s, the bouquet had

A bride's posey bouquet trimmed with point lace around the edge and tied with satin ribbons. (Godey's Lady's Book, 1872)

The posey remained the bridal bouquet of choice well into the mid-Victorian years, although it increased in size as the century wore on. This bouquet was created by Ellen McClelland Lesser for our Hermitage wedding breakfast. (Photograph by GF Studio / Rob Kern)

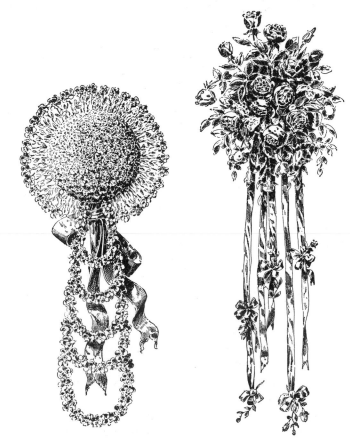

The bridal chatelaine could be made of roses or smaller flowers such as violets. (Ladies' Home Journal, 1891)

become so large that brides often left it at home to be held during the reception and instead carried a white prayer book during the church ceremony. Two famous brides, Princess May of Teck who married in 1893 the Duke of York (who later became King George V of England), and Consuelo Vanderbilt who married the Duke of Marlborough in 1895, carried enormous bouquets that established the trend for bridal sprays. The Vanderbilt bouquet of orchids, lilies of the valley, and ferns measured almost three feet across. Princess May's bouquet was more in the style of a fountain, wide across the top and cascading to the edge of her skirt. It was made up of the "House of York" rose, white orchids, lilies of the valley, a new carnation named "The Bride," and the traditional orange blossoms, of course.

One intermediate phase in the evolution of the bridal bouquet from posey to spray was the chatelaine. It was an appealing idea because it could be created with almost any flower. For the traditional bride, the chatelaine was made of white roses and green foliage with a cluster of roses in the center and single roses flaring out toward the edges. Long narrow ribbons with rosebuds knotted here and there in a seemingly casual way hung from under the central bunch.

For the bride who preferred dainty flowers such as violets, the same effect was created by arranging them in a tight round bouquet surrounded by an edging of single flowers. Chains of the same flower were then fastened to one another and suspended from the central bouquet. A broad ribbon bow was tied around the base.

Regardless of its style and size, the ribbons on the bridal bouquet played a significant role. If there were streamers, there had to be at least three knots for good luck. The knots represented man, wife, and child. Or, two streamers tied together could symbolize the union of two people in love. The ribbon of a smaller posey bouquet might be tied with a true lover's knot, since this was the symbol of eternity.

Throughout the era, it was the groom's responsibility to pay for the bride's bouquet.

After the wedding reception, before the bride and groom left on their wedding trip, it was customary for her to give each bridesmaid a flower from her bouquet. Sometimes a group of small individual arrangements

A bouquet for an 1895 bride created with bridal roses by Ellen McClelland Lesser. It is oval in outline with a rounded profile. At least two dozen roses are needed to achieve the full effect. (Photograph by G F Studio / Rob Kern)

The headpiece, to which the bridal veil was attached as in this example, was often created from orange blossoms. (Photograph by G F Studio / Rob Kern)

were tied together with ribbon to form the bridal bouquet. When the ribbon was untied, each bridesmaid received a small bouquet, one of which had hidden in it a gold ring that meant that the one lucky enough to receive it would become the next bride.

How this custom evolved into that of catching the bride's bouquet to determine which bridesmaid would be married next is unclear. During the 1870s, the individual bouquets tied together were thrown by some brides after the ribbon that held them was loosened, but only one of them was significant: the one with the ring. Later, the bride's bouquet was thrown into the group of relatives and friends waiting for the bride and groom to leave on their honeymoon to distract them, so that they could not be followed.

In addition to the flowers in her bouquet, the Victorian bride also wore flowers on her head. In the early days, they formed a coronet to which her veil was attached. Toward the middle and late years, as the coiffure became elaborate and the hair was arranged high on the head, one or two blossoms or a spray of flowers became more fashionable. Many times, as with the coronet of the earlier period, the flower of choice was the orange blossom, although roses were also favored.

One innovation that brides began to use after the middle of the century was the corsage bouquet. If the bride was carrying a prayer book, she might wear a posey of flowers, such as orange blossoms, on the corsage of her gown. These were known as corsage bouquets and were also worn by the bridesmaids at some weddings.

Dressing for the Wedding

The Bridegroom and His Attendants

Proper dress for the wedding was as much a concern for the bridegroom and his attendants as it was for the bride and the bridesmaids. They wanted to be dressed in the newest fashion and they wanted whatever they wore to be correct. Advice came from many sources, including the ladies' magazines as well as the men's.

In 1861, the *Ministers Gazette of Fashion* recommended that the bridegroom wear a frock coat of blue, claret, or mulberry. His waistcoat was to be white, possibly quilted, and his trousers of lavender doeskin. Black was not recommended. The best man and the groomsmen were also to wear frock coats, but in a color more subdued than that of the groom's coat.

Morning coat   *Frock coat*   *Full dress for evening*

The *West End Gazette of Fashion* in 1869 described a short frock coat of blue cloth with a velvet collar edged in silk cord. This had a waistcoat of white drill and trousers of dove gray. The gloves were lavender and the tie a light blue.

In the early Victorian era, the bridegroom, the best man, and the other male attendants would have worn a floral favor in their lapel, since by 1840 some men's frock coats had a buttonhole tailored for this purpose. By 1865, the "flower-hole," as it was called, had become quite common.

The frontier groom also wore a flower favor on the lapel of his best suit, using whatever flowers were in bloom at the time of the wedding. His flower was the same as the flowers carried by the bride.

By the mid-Victorian years, some fashionable journals, like *The Tailor and the Cutter*, stated that "Frock coats are seldom worn, even at weddings. The Morning Coat being preferred on account of its smarter appearance." However, not all of the social authorities agreed. The frock coat and vest of black cloth was still considered proper. It was to be worn with dark gray mixed trousers, a folded cravat of medium color, and lavender gloves stitched in black. If the bride was to be married in a traveling dress, the groom was still expected to wear a frock coat, not a business suit.

Harper's Bazar in 1885 stated that gloves could be omitted if the bridegroom chose not to wear them, but by 1886 it had reversed its stand and decreed that gentlemen in the wedding party must wear gloves, preferably a pale pearl color embroidered with black.

By 1899, fashion had changed again. This time *The Tailor and the Cutter* reported that the black frock coat was back in fashion.

With this, the groom was to wear a double-breasted, light-colored waistcoat, a dark tie, gray striped cashmere trousers, patent-leather button boots, and pale tan kid gloves. At all times, he was to carry a black silk top hat.

Those gentlemen who were confident enough to lead rather than follow fashion even wore colored shirts at daytime weddings. At one, a stylish young man wore a pink shirt with white collar and cuffs under his frock coat.

The boutonnieres at this time were large. They could be a bunch of lilies of the valley, a gardenia, or stephanotis. The Duke of Marlborough, at his wedding to Consuelo Vanderbilt, wore a large gardenia.

If the wedding was in the evening, full dress with tailcoats was in order, including white gloves. The traditional groom wore a white waistcoat, but for those who were more adventurous, *Harper's Bazar* in January 1890 reported that embroidered black silk was the newest and most "swagger thing." The father of the bride wore the same dress as the groom and his attendants. Gentlemen guests dressed according to the time of the wedding: morning dress during the day, full dress in the evening.

The Bridesmaids and The Maid of Honor

To be a bridesmaid or a maid of honor was the next best thing to being a bride. Young Victorian ladies invited to be attendants enjoyed the many hours spent with the bride discussing what they would wear.

The gowns needed to be practical as well as beautiful, for they would become part of their personal wardrobes afterwards. The thoughtful bride was aware of this and weighed personal preferences as well as the impact of the bridal party as a whole. If she was providing the costumes for the bridesmaids, and some did, the bride had more discretion in what they would wear.

During the early Victorian days when skirts were full and the bodice tiny, the bridal attendants, as well as the bride, wore white. To cover their heads, which was required if the wedding was to be in church, they had short white veils that fell from a coronet to just below the hip.

Although tradition called for white gowns, color in combination with white, or even an occasional dress of another color was perfectly proper as long as the silhouette was feminine and the overall effect was that of a white wedding.

In its "Centre Table Gossip" column, *Godey's* in 1861 gave a description of a bridesmaid's dress created by a fashionable dressmaker, which was white tulle with a rose-color silk slip underneath. A bertha on the bodice was pointed front and back with two rows of tulle ruches, trimmed at regular intervals with bows of rose-colored

A wedding in the country. (**The Girl's Own Paper,** *July 30, 1887*)

This bouquet for a bridesmaid in an 1870 wedding was created by Ellen McClelland Lesser. Bouquets of that time were basically white but also had some color. The bouquet is finished with a fringe of maidenhair fern and a paper frill. (Photograph by G F Studio / Rob Kern)

ribbon. Both the overskirt and the slip repeated the tulle ruches mixed with the same rose-color bow-ribbons. The veil was surmounted by a wreath of red and white roses. It was a pretty combination that was predominantly white, with enough color in the accents to achieve a romantic look.

That same issue of *Godey's* featured "a decided novelty—coiffure for a bridesmaid." Actually there were two. One had the hair banded closely with a handsome ivory or silver comb, a bandeau composed of a ruche of double crepe, with bouquets of pansies, and a short illusion veil flowing gracefully down over the neck. The other was suggested for a bridesmaid at a reception or wedding party. It was a wreath of ribbon loops, blue, pink, or rose with black lace between, terminating in a flat bow with floating ends.

A few years later, in January 1867, *Godey's* had two dresses for bridesmaids in its fashion plate for brides. One was white; the other green.

The white one was silk with an over-dress of white crepe, looped and trimmed with flowers. It had a plain corsage with a bertha formed of folds of crepe edged with lace. Festoons of flowers were draped both on the front and the back of the corsage as well as on the skirt. These fragile-looking flowers only served to enhance the feminine silhouette. The girdle was gold.

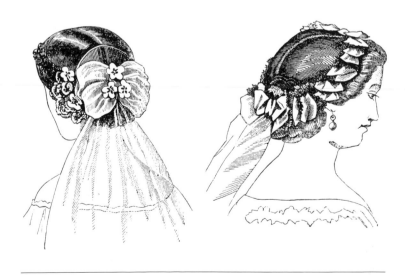

Coiffures and headdresses for a bridesmaid from **Godey's,** *December 1861.*

Godey's *Fashions for January 1867.*

The green silk was simpler in design, although it, too, had a gold girdle. It was made with a peplum that was quite short in the front, running down to sharp points finished with tassels at the side of the skirt. The corsage, which had a square neckline, was shaped with pleats in what was known as the Greek form. It was trimmed with velvet and finished with point lace.

The headdress for the first one was a coronet of flowers from which fell a tulle veil, and for the second, bands of green velvet. Since there was no veil for this one, it may have been intended for a wedding at home.

Mid-Victorian bridesmaids, like the bride, more than likely wore a gown with a bustle. It was the height of fashion. Although white was not necessarily the traditional color for bridesmaids during this period, it was still worn at some weddings, often in combination with another color. The choice depended, in part, on what the fashion news was for each season. At one wedding in 1874, the bridesmaids wore gowns that had white skirts and pink bodices.

Nellie Grant's bridesmaids were dressed in white silk, with the color accent in the flowers they carried. Four had bouquets of pink flowers and four had bouquets of blue flowers.

At the Lawler-Sturges wedding of 1886 in Prairie Du Chien, Wisconsin, the three bridesmaids wore short (just above the floor) dresses of white surah and lace with leghorn hats trimmed with wild roses, and they carried bouquets of pink buds.

Society reports were avidly read by young ladies in order to obtain ideas for their own weddings. In one account of December 1885, the four bridesmaids wore short costumes of white silk trimmed with sable fur and close round bonnets of white lace without strings. In 1885, "short" meant floor-length, not knee-length. They carried large bunches of rich roses.

At another fashionable wedding the bridesmaids' dresses were of white brocaded satin with a deep band of Russian sable on the skirt and a sable fichu around the neck that crossed over to the left of the bodice. Their small bonnets were of white velvet with a border of fur on the brim and at the end of the crown.

During this period, some brides took their inspirations from paintings in order to create a romantic wedding scene. The shepherdess look from a Watteau painting was the inspiration for one bride who chose dotted muslin trimmed with lace for the bridesmaids, and to complete the picture, big inverted hat baskets tied with long satin streamers that the bridesmaids were to carry, each of which was filled with a different flower.

For the spring of 1886, the fashion editors recommended point d'esprit for a bridesmaid's dress. It was a net fabric with exceedingly small dots. With this they suggested a scallop-edged lace with equally small dots for the trim. The dress was white, designed with yellow ribbon bows placed in ladder fashion on one side, or if the young lady preferred, a yellow watered-ribbon sash could be worn at the waist. Her flowers had to be yellow to match the accent, either a bouquet of yellow roses, or a small posey of long-stemmed jonquils worn on the corsage of the dress.

By the 1890s, the Victorians were less dependent on rigid rules for weddings and more willing to try novelties in dress. This is not to say that fashion in dress was not important. It was, especially the news from Paris and

A white point d'esprit dress with a bustle for the mid-Victorian bridesmaid. (**Harper's Bazar**, 1882)

A bridesmaid's dress for a pink and white wedding. (**Ladies' Home Journal**, *June 1891*)

A bouquet for an 1895 bridesmaid made of Bridal Pink roses by Ellen McClelland Lesser. The bouquet also contains pink sweetheart roses. The streamers are of a pale green ribbon with a rosebud knotted here and there along the length of the ribbon. (Photograph by GF Studio/Rob Kern)

large or very tiny, or embroidered with rose garlands above the hem and smaller flowers scattered above. They also liked crepe de chine and soft repped bengaline in the princess style. The hat suggested for any of these fabrics was a low-crowned straw trimmed with spring blossoms, with the brim faced with a shirred crepe in the color being accented in the gown.

In the June 1891 issue, the *Ladies' Home Journal* featured a bridesmaid's dress for a pink-and-white wedding that could be worn after the wedding for afternoon or evening affairs, or even at fashionable watering places. The skirt was plain, the length being two inches above the floor. Three slashes at the edge were caught up with white ribbon. A figured material was used for the bodice and then arranged in small paniers over the hips. The back of the skirt was in the princess fashion, undraped. As was the fashion then, full sleeves were set high on the shoulder, narrowing at the elbow where they were finished with pointed cuffs edged with deep frills of lace. With this, white undressed-kid gloves were to extend under the sleeves so that no bare arm would show. The throat was finished with a full frill of chiffon.

The hair was arranged low on the neck and tied with a pink ribbon. The hat was of white Neapolitan straw, bent in waves with a cluster of pink orchids on top. A bouquet of orchids tied with a long pink satin ribbon was suggested. Although it featured pink to contrast with the basically white dress, the *Ladies' Home Journal* assured its readers that any color they fancied could be substituted for the pink.

That same issue of the *Ladies' Home Journal* pictured a bride and her maid of honor in dresses that complemented one another in line and design. The maid of honor had a dress of lightweight white silk with a narrow yellow stripe. The edge of the skirt had a frill of lace caught at intervals with knots of yellow ribbon. The gown was fitted in what was known as the apron style, with the yoke portion above the bib being of white silk with printed yellow roses. The edge of the bib was outlined with gold passementerie. The top of the sleeves had full caps of lace over the white silk with the printed yellow rose. Her large straw hat was decorated with yellow ribbon and white roses and she carried a bouquet of yellow flowers.

New York, but so were the innovations that those with status made fashionable.

The major change in style was the emphasis on the shoulder, with sleeves that were very wide and high on the top and fitted like a sheath on the lower arm. There were many variations of this large sleeve. Some were artificially supported with layers of wadding, hair cloth, and even light steel springs, all to create the wide shoulder silhouette that was the current mode.

Harper's Bazar for Spring 1890 reported that gray, violet, and lilac were the colors being suggested by English modistes, but that in America the preference was for white, rose, or green. Some of the fashionable fabrics were mousseline de soie, with spots that were either very

A bride and her maid of honor in dresses that complement one another. (**Ladies' Home Journal,** *June 1891*)

In the fall of 1898, *Harper's Bazar* stated that the Paris fashions for brides were smarter than ever and recommended that the costumes of bridesmaids and the maid of honor be in sharp contrast to the bride so as not to detract from the beauty of her gown. One of the newest fashions for bridesmaids that season was mousseline de soie designed to give the effect of an overskirt with a very wide and long flounce of rows of tucking underneath. Three rows of Valenciennes lace on the overskirt repeated the lines created by the tucks. The waist had a yoke of tiny pleats with the same lace trim. Over this was a bertha of mousseline de soie, trimmed with a ruffle and finished with a rosette. Although the sleeves were puffed at the top, they were not as exaggerated as some. The wrists were finished with a deep pleated ruffle.

Costumes for bridesmaids in 1898 were to be in sharp contrast to the bride so as not to detract from the beauty of her gown. (**Harper's Bazar,** *October 8, 1898*)

For her headdress, the fashion editors suggested a hat of felt or white chenille braid covered with white roses and leaves, or if she preferred, a small toque.

Although the style of the dresses might be alike, not all bridesmaids wore the same color. When it was fashionable to have twelve attendants, as in the late 1890s, some brides chose to have them dress in different colors, with each two walking together down the aisle to be wearing the same color. Or, they might be dressed in graduating shades of the same color.

For example, Miss Marie Weed Alden, whose marriage to Henry J. Davison in Millbrook, New York, in 1891 was one of the prominent weddings of the season, patterned the tableau of her wedding after a famous painting. The bridesmaids had dresses made in Marie Antoinette style with Watteau trains, each in a different color: pale green, old rose, white, and yellow. The maid of honor wore white satin with brocaded roses. The gowns had a low-cut neck with a long flounce of Duchess lace surrounding it.

At an eight o'clock evening wedding in Brooklyn, New York, in 1890, the bridesmaids for Miss Marion Isabel Smith wore pink silk gowns with a drapery of chiffon and carried daisies. The maid of honor wore lavender silk and carried a bouquet of pink roses.

In Grand Rapids, Michigan, in 1897, when Amanda Voigt married Charles Perkins in a wedding at home, the maid of honor wore a handsome gown of pink satin with a demitrain, trimmed with ruchings of mousseline de soie. One bridesmaid wore an accordion-pleated Liberty silk over pink taffeta with trimmings of Duchess lace and another wore a gown of white mousseline de soie over pink taffeta with ruchings of pink taffeta.

Another bride, Virginia Dousman of Prairie Du Chien, Wisconsin, in 1904 chose to have all her attendants dressed in white chiffon trimmed with white Irish lace. They wore white Irish-lace hats with pompoms and streamers and carried "old-fashioned" nosegays tied with tulle, and with long tulle streamers.

The maid of honor wore a Directoire costume of white faille silk and lace and a Directoire white lace hat with large plumes. She carried a nosegay of pink rosebuds, tied like those carried by the bridesmaids.

Whatever the circumstances, the bridesmaids' gowns were expected to be less grand than that of the bride.

The Children

Not only was the participation of children in the Victorian wedding party symbolic, it also added considerable charm and grace, provided they were well-bred and well-behaved.

Little girls could be flower girls, or ring bearers. Those somewhat older could be junior bridesmaids or young maids of honor. They usually carried baskets of flowers rather than bouquets and walked directly in front of, or immediately in back of the bride.

Regardless of their role, quite often they were dressed in white muslin tied with a ribbon sash that matched their shoes and stockings. Thus, they might wear blue shoes and stockings with a blue sash, pink shoes and stockings with a pink ribbon sash, or if it was a wedding at Christmastime, red shoes, red stockings, and a red ribbon sash. Their skirts were short or long, depending on the prevailing styles, and the ages of the girls. If appropriate, they wore large brimmed hats, or perhaps a crown of flowers. Of course, each wedding was unique and the costumes for the little girls varied with the theme selected by the bride.

The costume for the little boys was more traditional. They were dressed as court pages and frequently walked behind the bride to hold her train. Their velvet jackets and short trousers could be black, blue, green, or red with a round linen collar fastened by a large bow of white crepe de chine or surah. Their laced shoes and long stockings were black, and, like the adult men, they wore light tan or pearl-color gloves.

If the costume was very formal, their trousers were white satin knee-breeches and the hose white silk. The laced shoes in this instance were to have shining buckles of silver, steel, or gold.

Ordinarily, they did not wear hats, but if they did, they were made of velvet to match their coats, with a white plume and a buckle like that worn on their shoes. These hats were to be removed when they entered the church.

Some weddings had two pages, others four. Depending on the tableau the bride wished to create, they could be dressed alike, or in different combinations of colors provided they did not repeat the hues worn by the bridesmaids.

The Mothers and the Guests

Social custom drew a fine line between what the mothers wore at a wedding and what was worn by the lady guests. It was a subtle difference that every proper Victorian woman was expected to know.

At a daytime wedding, the "correct" attire for a guest was a walking or visiting costume, in the newest fashion colors and silhouettes. The mothers (and other female members of both families), on the other hand, were expected to dress in reception toilettes. These were more elegant than the daytime costumes of the guests, but less formal than evening dress.

If the wedding was to be in church, both the mothers and the guests were expected to wear bonnets. For an at-home wedding, bonnets were optional, and at an evening wedding they were not considered appropriate. *Harper's Bazar* of 1890 did make one exception to this rule. If the guest was an "elderly and delicate" lady, she could wear a handsome bonnet with a gown that had a train or a headdress made from lace, ostrich tips, and ribbon fastened by jeweled hairpins.

Within these parameters, there was ample opportunity, both for the mothers and the guests, to choose from among the styles and colors of the season. Not all the sources they normally turned to for ideas were that helpful. Although fashion journals often mentioned specific trends for brides and bridesmaids, they seldom mentioned the mother of the bride, let alone the mother of the groom. Those who were resourceful created their own toilette. Others wrote to magazine editors for advice.

In answer to a query from a mother of the groom, regarding a June wedding, the *Ladies' Home Journal* suggested a gown of black mousseline de soie and lace made up over white silk, or a gown of pale gray voile with trimmings of black lace. For either gown, a bonnet of white and black tulle could be worn. Black silk or black net were often recommended for the mothers by *Harper's*

Early Victorian reception dress.

Reception toilettes for mid-Victorian weddings. (Harper's Bazar, 1886)

Bazar in the late Victorian era. These fashion fabrics, although they were black, were not to be confused with black crepe, which was a denser fabric that signified mourning.

At weddings in families where the mother was in mourning, she was expected to put her mourning crepe aside for the ceremony and to appear in color. In America, purple velvet or silk were considered proper. The English preferred a cardinal red.

In 1874, when Nellie Grant, the daughter of President Ulysses S. Grant, was married to Algernon C.F. Sartoris in the White House, Mrs. Grant, who was in mourning for her father, wore a mauve-color silk dress trimmed with ruffles of black lace.

Back of gown

Reception costume for a late Victorian wedding. (Harper's Bazar, 1898)

Wedding toilettes: mother, bride, bridesmaid. (Harper's Bazar, *1886)*

At a very distinguished society wedding in Dubuque, Iowa, in 1874, both mothers wore black silk, trimmed in lace, with pond lilies in their hair. It was a late afternoon wedding.

In November 1891, at the Davidson-Alden wedding in Millbrook, New York, the mother of the bride wore black velvet and jet with a court train lined in white satin, caught with white ostrich feathers. The neck was low and the waist sleeveless. The newspaper account said that she had worn this same dress for her presentation at the Court of St. James's.

All mothers, however, didn't choose to wear black.

Brooklyn Life of April 26, 1890 reported that the mother of the bride at the marriage of a Miss Carrie A. Tuttle was gowned in pearl-color brocade trimmed with Duchess lace and steel passementerie, and wore diamond ornaments. And in April 1892, that same paper noted that the bride's mother at an evening wedding wore an elegant gown of récedé satin and brocade trimmed with point lace. She, too, wore diamond ornaments.

Queen Victoria, who was the mother of the bride or the groom more than once, always wore black and white because she was in mourning for her "dearest Albert."

• 43 •

A late Victorian bride and her mother.
(Harper's Bazar, 1896)

The Marriage Ceremony

Illustrated London News, *November 3, 1883*

To the Victorians, there was a fine distinction between a marriage and a wedding. The former was the religious ceremony that united a couple in heart and hand, presumably forever, while the latter comprised the social activities preceding and following it.

The marriage ceremony could take place in church or at home, depending partly on the religious preference of the family. If it was to be in a sanctuary, social custom declared that it should be in the church attended by the bride's family, not only to respect their dignity, but also because it was proper for a bride to go to her husband from her habitual house of worship. The church service could be public with many guests in attendance, or private with just family and a few intimate friends, even if there was to be a festive wedding breakfast afterwards.

Flowers for the Wedding

Flowers were an integral part of the Victorian wedding. Usually, one flower was designated as a theme for the wedding, chosen because of the sentiment associated with it.

Here are some of the more frequently used flowers and their meanings:

Orange Blossom	Chastity: your purity equals your loveliness
Lily of the Valley	Return of happiness
Lilac	Humility and purity
White Daisy	Beauty and innocence
White Chrysanthemum	Cheerfulness and truth
Bridal Rose	Happy love
Blue Violet	Love
Honeysuckle	The bond of love
Apple Blossom	Preference
Tulip	Declaration of love

The one flower that was not used in the later years was the tuberose, for its perfume was considered too sickening. Since most weddings also had a color scheme, the flowers really played a dual role. In the early years, yellow was avoided because it was associated with jealousy. In the later years, this stigma had disappeared and yellow was quite popular. So, too, was pink.

Some brides carried out the one-flower theme in all the details of their wedding, including the design of the lace they wore, the embroidery on their gown, and even a brooch depicting that flower was chosen as a gift for their bridesmaids. Those who were especially sentimental made the flower of the wedding their special flower for life.

Decorating the Church

If the marriage ceremony was to take place in church, the decorations could be as simple as potted palms and baskets of white flowers or as profuse as the family's finances would permit. By the mid-Victorian years, lavish floral decorations were preferred and by the end of the era, elaborate designs became fashionable.

For instance, evergreens were entwined with the flower of choice and used as festoons from the ceiling to the galleries at the side of the church. These same ropes of greens and flowers were wrapped around the altar rails and pillars, outlined the pulpit, and even formed arches over the aisle for the bridal party to pass through on the way to the altar.

White ribbons tied in bows on standards at the end of every few pews were used in St. Luke's Episcopal Church in Brooklyn. Another decoration that was used in the First Baptist Church of Los Angeles, California, was a canopy covered with pepper-tree foliage with a bell of pink geraniums suspended from it, lighted by electricity. And in St. Paul's Episcopal Church in San Diego, California, Easter lilies, yellow and white roses, and marguerites were combined with smilax and English ivy.

One charming decoration used occasionally at church weddings was a low gateway of flowers and greenery at the entrance to the altar. At the proper moment in the ceremony, a young member of the bridal party came forward to open it for the bride and groom to

When the wedding was at home, the draperies were drawn to darken the room so that the lights from the gas jets or electric lamps (for those who had electricity) could cast a soft glow. This is the parlor at Adsmore as it was decorated for the wedding of Selina Smith and John Osborne. (Photograph by Martin Studio. Princeton, Kentucky)

enter. When Mayme Smith married R.D. Garrett in 1892, there were two passageways to the altar in the First Presbyterian Church in Princeton, Kentucky. Each was closed by a gate of wire wrapped with passion vine and interwoven with chrysanthemums, since this was the flower theme for the wedding. In the semicircle formed by the arch just above each gate were placed the initials "S" and "G"—"S" over the gate through which the bride would pass and "G" over the gate for the groom. It was a beautiful scene.

Among striking floral decorations at the marriage of Consuelo Vanderbilt and the Duke of Marlborough in 1895 were the tall stanchions, placed at the end of every fifth pew on the center aisle in the church, which held bouquets of roses and greens that were four feet high.

When Ellen McClelland Lesser decorated our room at The Hermitage for the wedding breakfast, she, of course, included the hearth. (Photograph by GF Studio/Rob Kern)

Decorating the House

Although it was less formal than a church setting, the wedding at home was equally proper and the decorations were no less abundant. Flowers in a profusion of white or the color theme chosen for the wedding were used throughout.

The ceremony usually took place in the drawing room. If there was a bay window, this was the natural place for an altar improvised from banks of palms and flowers. A good-luck symbol made entirely of white flowers was suspended over the spot where the bride and groom would stand. This could be a wedding bell, a wishbone, a horseshoe, or a dove with a ring in its beak. An innovation introduced in 1883 was borrowed from the Japanese. It was an umbrella of flowers that was supposed to be a lucky emblem for the newly married couple because it would protect them from stones, hail, and evil spirits.

At the Voigt-Perkins wedding in Grand Rapids, Michigan, in 1897, the improvised altar was banked with

Easter lilies with a canopy of Easter lilies and smilax suspended above it. The color theme was pink and white with palms and hydrangeas predominating. The mantel shelf in one room was banked with Paris daisies, in another with hydrangea and spirea. The mirrors and chandeliers were wrapped with garlands of spirea and hydrangea, and even the bookshelves were outlined with ropes of greens and flowers.

The bridal way down the stairs to the drawing room was outlined by a row of tiny electric lamps that glittered among the surrounding foliage. The remainder of the way from the bottom of the stairs to the altar was lined with white ribbon, held, no doubt, by the ushers.

The windows in the room used for a wedding reception would have been decorated with flowers. (Photograph by GF Studio/Rob Kern)

Decorations in the home were not limited, however, to traditional wedding flowers. Wild flowers such as Queen Anne's lace and goldenrod were used when they were in season.

For the November 1891 Davidson-Alden wedding in Millbrook, New York, a society florist used cornstalks, pumpkins, rye, and wheat to bank over the mantelpieces, around the pier glasses, and in the corners of the halls, accenting them with fancy ribbons.

At some home wed- dings, even the windows and doors were decorated. The *Ladies' Home Journal* of 1895 gave instructions for several designs. One was a floral curtain for a window or a door that was made from strings of leaves or flowers hung from a pole across the top. These "cur- tains" were looped back with white ribbons. In the space above the pole, a basket hoop wound with flowers framed a marriage bell.

The *Journal's* instructions for the marriage bell were as follows:

> A marriage bell is made in the following manner: Take three hoops of diminishing sizes and hang together with strings or wire—the largest hoop at the bottom, the smallest at the top. Cover with leaves, and line with white or yellow bunting. Hang an electric light inside. The suspended lamp should be artistically and attractively covered with leaves, and suspended so as to serve as a tongue to the floral marriage bell.

They also recommended framing pictures and sconces on the walls with wreaths of leaves tied with long white ribbons. For those who wanted advice on which flowers to use, the editor offered these suggestions:

> Holly or laurel can be used for decorations during every month in the year except June, July, and August. Ferns can be used for these three summer months. Southern smilax and palms are always to be obtained. Flowers for December, January, February, and March are Marguerite daisies, carnations, and violets; April, carnations, lilies, and violets; May will add asparagus ferns, sweet alyssum, and tulips; June, hollyhocks, daisies, and peonies; July, goldenrod; August, asters; September, October, and November, chrysanthemums, dahlias, and autumn foliage; and roses at all times.

The Church Ceremony

Most church weddings were formal, with all the traditional rituals that made it such a romantic event. It was one of the greatest moments in a girl's life and every decision leading up to it was measured against the social standards of the period.

One usher was selected by the bride to be the master of ceremonies in the church. This meant that he was to get to the church early, arrange for the spreading of the carpet from the church door to the pavement, calculate the space needed for the seating of the more important guests, and place a ribbon or arch of flowers to designate the reserved area. In addition, he was to see that the organist was present, that the program of compositions was correctly arranged, and that the kneeling stools for the bride and groom were in their proper places. These were usually covered with white fabric and could be quite elaborate, some even embroidered in pearls.

At very formal weddings in large cities such as New York, especially in the late 1880s and 1890s, it was also the responsibility of the master of ceremonies to make certain that no one without a card of admission entered. This was so rigidly enforced that those ladies who needed to bring their servants with them to the church were issued extra cards in advance.

Meanwhile, the other ushers went to the bride's home for last-minute instructions and for their wedding favors, if it was in the 1840s–1860s, or for their bouton- nieres of flowers if it was later. According to custom, it was the bride who fastened these to the lapels of their coats.

Wedding favors made of white ribbon, lace, flowers, and silver leaves were an English custom that was not universally accepted in America. Prince Albert as well as other grooms of the royal family in England wore white ribbon bows as favors on their shoulders when they were married. American grooms preferred the boutonniere. Guests and servants wore them to identify with the wedding. At earlier Victorian weddings, favors were made by the bridesmaids and placed in the vestry of the church where they could be pinned on the sleeves and shoulders of guests after the ceremony. Later in the era, they were worn by servants taking part in the festivities, such as the coachmen and footmen of the carriages. These favors were usually large bunches of white ribbons and flowers. Even the ears of the horses were decorated with them. In the English tradition, on her wedding day, those servants who had known the bride from the time that she was a little girl expected her to fasten to their garments a favor that she had personally made. It was also a custom to present a small gratuity such as a new dress or cap or box of cake as a favor to each one.

After the ushers had received their boutonnieres from the bride, they went directly to the church so that they could carry out their duties to escort the guests to their proper seats.

If the guest's name was not on a list prepared for him by the bride, the usher would inquire, as he offered his right arm to the lady, whether she was a friend of the bride or the groom. If a friend of the bride, she was taken to a seat on the left side of the aisle; if a friend of the groom, to the right side. When the lady was escorted by a gentleman, he was to follow her to the seat. How close each guest was seated to the altar depended on the relationship to the bride or groom. Those not related were seated in back of the white ribbon that the master of ceremonies had placed earlier to mark the reserved spaces.

Guests who were in mourning were to enter the church quietly and to hide themselves in the crowd to escape the eyes of the bridal couple, since to the superstitious Victorians, the sight of mourning crepe by the bridal couple was a bad omen.

While the guests were arriving for the marriage ceremony, the best man was in the vestry with the groom, providing moral support. His principal responsibilities were the business and social formalities of the wedding.

During the ceremony he was to hold the groom's top hat and gloves, and to see that he had the wedding ring in his pocket. Traditionally, this was a plain gold band engraved inside with the initials of the bride and groom and the date of the wedding. If the wedding ring was dropped during the ceremony, it was considered good luck because all the evil spirits were thus shaken out of it. Although some weddings were double-ring ceremonies, at many, especially in the 1890s, only the bride received a ring.

In the 1880s and later, it was customary for the maid of honor and the bridesmaids to arrive at the church with the bride. Before that, in the 1870s, the bridesmaids had escorts called groomsmen (because they had been selected by the groom) to call at their homes to take them to the church and to be their cavaliers at the wedding. Bridesmaids had no specific responsibilities per se. However, during the weeks preceding the wedding these friends of the bride were very much involved in giving luncheons for her, helping her select her trousseau, gossiping in anticipation of the big day, and preparing the wedding favors. After the wedding, as a courtesy, one or more were expected to call upon the mother of the bride daily while her daughter was away on her honeymoon.

The maid of honor did have a distinct role in the wedding. She preceded the bride down the aisle, stood next to her during the ceremony and held her bouquet. Sometimes she was also designated to help the bride with final touches to her bridal toilette, for another Victorian superstition held that a bride should not finish dressing until just before she left for the church.

The Bridal Procession

The bridal procession in the 1870s and 1880s was very formal in its organization and procedure.

Our Deportment, in 1880, called for the bridesmaids, each linked to the arm of a groomsman, to walk up the aisle first. When they reached the first step of the altar, the ladies were to go to the left, the gentlemen to the right. The ushers followed in pairs, just ahead of the groom, who walked in the procession with the bride's mother on his arm. After seating her in the front pew at the left, he joined the groomsmen to wait for the bride. Next came the bride on the arm of her father (or next of kin). He was to wait at her left, a step or two in back of her until asked to give her away. At that point, he took her right hand and gave it to the clergyman who in turn placed it in the hand of the groom. The father then joined the mother of the bride in her pew.

If there were no ushers or bridesmaids, the procedure was as follows.

The members of the bride's family preceded the bride to the church. She followed with her mother. When they arrived, the groom awaited them and gave his arm to the bride's mother and walked up the aisle with her to the altar. Here the bride's mother stepped back and slightly to the left, and the groom turned to face the aisle as the bride came down with her father. When they had reached the altar, the bride joined the groom and the father stepped back to the left to join her mother.

The relatives followed, taking their places standing; those of the bride to the left, those of the groom to the right. After kneeling at the altar for a moment, the bride standing on the left of the bridegroom took the glove from off her left hand, while he took the glove from off his right hand and the service began. The father of the bride, when asked who giveth her away, was to bow rather than stepping forward to put her hand in that of the clergyman. It was expected that "Perfect self-control should be exhibited by all parties during the ceremony."

After the ceremony, the bride was to take the bridegroom's arm and they were to go back down the aisle without looking to the right or the left. It was considered to be in very bad taste to recognize acquaintances by bows and smiles while in church.

That same year *Our Deportment* also noted the latest New York form for the bridal procession:

When the bridal party has arranged itself for entrance, the ushers, in pairs, march slowly up to the altar, and turn to the right. Behind them follows the groom alone. When he reaches the altar he turns, faces the aisle, and watches intently for the coming of his bride. After a slight interval the bridesmaids follow, in pairs, and at the altar turn to the left. After another brief interval, the bride, alone and entirely veiled, with her eyes cast down, follows her companions. The groom comes forward a few steps to meet

her, takes her hand, and places her at the altar. Both kneel for a moment's silent devotion. The parents of the bride, having followed her, stand just behind her and partly to the left. The services by the clergyman now proceed as usual.

A decade later, the procedure began to change, for there was more willingness to innovate. The bridal procession and the grouping of the bridal party at the altar were looked upon as a tableau that should be arranged for the most beautiful effect. Some brides even tried to recreate a painting in the colors they had selected for the bridesmaids.

Usually, these innovations were first made by socially prominent brides in cities such as New York, and Boston, and then adopted by middle-class Victorian brides who read about them in the ladies' magazines.

At the Smith-Garrett wedding in Princeton, Kentucky, in 1892, the two passageways to the altar were closed by two gates covered with flowers. As the procession began, each gate was opened by a little girl. The bride and her bridesmaids passed down the left aisle; the groom and his best man down the right. They walked through the gates and met in front of the rostrum, at which point the minister joined the group and the two little girls closed the gates. When the ceremony was over, the bridal party left through the groom's gate.

At another wedding with ten bridesmaids, five from each side of the chancel came together, walked up the aisle in pairs to meet the bride at the church door, and then turned and preceded her back down the aisle.

Still another innovation had the ushers and bridesmaids walk down the side aisles, while the maid of honor, the bride, and her father came down the center aisle. They all met at the chancel.

One bride, who had no attendants, chose to walk down the aisle alone, preceded by her parents walking arm in arm.

Many brides liked to have small children participate in the wedding procession because the Victorians believed that they would ensure a fruitful marriage. Little girls walking just in front of the bride carried baskets of flower petals which they scattered in her path on the way to the altar. At the Lawler-Sturgis wedding in 1886, the bride's little niece carried her bouquet, escorted by her cousin who was dressed as a page. Sometimes bridesmaids under the age of ten followed the adult bridesmaids. Little boys dressed as pages held the bride's train, or walked in the procession carrying sheaves of wheat as symbols of fertility. Either girls or boys could be ring bearers, and they sometimes carried the ring on a silver salver rather than on a pillow.

The entrance of the groom was more traditional. If the groom had not escorted the bride's mother to her seat, he and the best man entered the church from the vestry and waited at the altar for the bride.

In addition to the Bridal March from Lohengrin, which was played while the bride walked to the altar, and Mendelssohn's Wedding March, played while the bride and groom came back down the aisle after being made husband and wife, the fully choral wedding became a fashionable innovation in the late Victorian era, both in England and America. This was an elaborate musical program integrated with the ceremony. A string ensemble played selections before the bridal procession began; a chorus of young choir boys rendered an epithalamion (a nuptial poem or song) as the bride walked down the aisle; the Hallelujah Chorus or some other choral music was offered during the service, and "Oh Perfect Love" was sung at the end. Newspaper accounts of these weddings always mentioned that they were fully choral, for it was considered impressive.

Once they had met at the altar, the bride and groom knelt for a moment of silent devotion, on very elaborate kneelers placed there for them. The maid of honor and the best man could also kneel with them. Then they would rise and the ceremony would begin. At this point, if the bride was carrying a prayer book, she handed it to the clergyman. If she had not opened the seam of the ring finger of her left glove, she removed it for the maid of honor to hold.

The wedding vows asked her to love, honor, and obey, and asked him to love and to cherish. If the groom was wealthy, the etiquette books say that he also added the words "With all my worldly goods I thee endow" so as to make the bride his equal. Some Victorian brides, like Queen Victoria, chose to leave the word "obey" in, while others like Susan B. Anthony had it omitted. President

Grover Cleveland in consideration for his young wife asked that the word "keep" be substituted for "obey."

Up to 1880, when the bride and groom had exchanged their vows and the clergyman had pronounced them man and wife, it was customary for the clergyman to kiss the bride before she turned to walk down the aisle. This custom came to be looked upon as an unwarranted liberty and was stopped because the Victorians in the later years did not believe that "an osculatory display" tied the knot any tighter. At the end of the ceremony, the maid of honor handed the bouquet back to the bride (if she had carried one), the best man handed the top hat and gloves to the groom, and the newlyweds marched down the aisle arm in arm followed by the bridal party. If the wedding took place in the second half of the Victorian era, the bride's veil was not lifted from her face until she had left the church. At earlier weddings, the veil was purely decorative, hanging from the back of her head.

At some weddings, while the clergyman was congratulating the newlyweds, little girls dressed in white appeared with baskets of rose petals, scattering them on the aisle from the altar to the carriage waiting for the bride and groom. Or, they stood up on the seats at the ends of the pews and tossed rose petals onto the entire bridal party as they walked down the aisle.

The father and mother of the bride were the first to leave the church after the ceremony. Meanwhile, the bride and groom were driven to the reception preferably in a white coach drawn by four white horses, as this was the English custom. The ushers rushed ahead to the house to be certain that everything was in readiness to receive them for the reception.

The best man was the last to leave the church. He had to present the fee for the service to the clergyman, which could range from ten dollars to hundreds of dollars, depending on the generosity of the groom. Five dollars was considered an absolute minimum in 1886 and twenty dollars acceptable for a person of moderate means. The organist also had to receive his fee. Twenty-five dollars was considered appropriate.

The Wedding Ceremony at Home

Some brides preferred to be married at home because it was more private. To create an intimate setting the draperies were drawn across the windows of the front parlor and any adjoining rooms so that lights from the gas lamps could cast a quiet glow (see illustration page 45).

The bride might be dressed in a formal wedding gown, or a traveling dress and bonnet, depending on the size of the affair. She could carry a bouquet, or wear a bouquet on the corsage of her dress.

If there were no attendants, the clergyman entered the parlor first, walked to the altar, and turned to face the guests. The bride and groom followed and took their places facing the clergyman. Then came her father, mother, and other close friends. Since there were no attendants, there was no need for anyone to give the bride away.

A wedding with attendants was somewhat more formal. The ushers formed an aisle with long white satin ribbons from the parlor door to the consecrated spot for the bridal party. The best man and groom entered, carrying their tall hats and white kid gloves. Then came the bridesmaids in pairs, the maid of honor, and then the bride on the arm of her father or next of kin. If there was only one bridesmaid as an attendant, she could be conducted to the improvised altar by a brother of the groom or some close friend, but never the best man. It was his responsibility to stay with the groom. When the bridal party was grouped in front of the clergyman, the groom handed his hat and gloves to the best man and then joined the bride.

After the ceremony, the minister congratulated the bride and groom and moved away, the best man handed his top hat and gloves back to the groom, and the newlyweds turned to face the room, with the bridesmaids on either side, ready to receive congratulations from the guests. The ushers at this point assumed their roles to escort and introduce the guests.

Quite often, home weddings were in the evening, anytime from five o'clock to eight o'clock or even nine. Although the ceremony was the same and the etiquette for congratulating the bride and groom did not differ from an earlier wedding, the dress for both the bridal party and the guests was more formal and the supper was lighter with less rich foods.

Pre-Wedding Activities

One practice that seems to have been more American than English was the rehearsal for the marriage ceremony, whether the wedding was to be in a church or at home. Especially in the 1890s when the grouping at the altar was thought of as a marriage tableau, one rehearsal, and maybe more, was considered necessary to ensure a beautiful arrangement. Ideally, it was scheduled several days before the wedding.

The bride set the date and wrote to each of the participants informing them of the details, including the distances each member of the bridal party should walk apart going down the aisle, the grouping at the altar, and the manner of departure after the service. This provided each of the party the means of learning their parts ahead of time. At the rehearsal one of her friends played the role of the bride, since the Victorians believed that it was bad luck for the bride to go through the ritual before the marriage took place.

In addition to the rehearsal, during the week of the wedding the bride gave a dinner or a luncheon for her bridesmaids and maid of honor, and the groom gave a bachelor dinner for his attendants.

Hers was a very feminine affair, with a display of her trousseau and talk of the wedding. The bride could, if she chose, present her souvenirs of the wedding to each of her attendants at this time. These were to be enduring novelties such as fans, rings, lockets, or miniature prayer books. If the wedding had a floral theme, such as a daisy wedding or a chrysanthemum wedding, she might present each with a pin with a diamond center representing the flower.

Some brides chose to invite the groom and the ushers to a dance after the dinner. If this hospitality was extended, then the bride's parents were expected to be present.

The groom's dinner, on the other hand, was usually given at a club or a hotel, and it was a stag affair. Inasmuch as selecting the attendants, including the ushers, was the privilege of the bride, this dinner also served as an opportunity for the groom to get to know them, especially if he was from another city. The groom sat at the head of the table and the best man opposite him. The clergyman was invited as a courtesy, but he usually declined, because his presence might lessen the merriment at the bachelor's last dinner.

The traditional groom's gift to his attendants was a scarf pin that he placed alongside a boutonniere for each at the table.

The stone for the scarf pin could represent the birthday of the bride or the groom, or if they believed in good luck charms, it could be a tiger's eye. Circumstances permitting, the stone was circled with diamonds.

During the course of the festivities, the groom and his attendants all drank a toast to the bride's health. Then, each broke his glass, so that it could never be put to a less honorable use.

The Wedding Breakfast

Throughout the Victorian era, the wedding breakfast was the most popular form of reception for the bride and groom. Queen Victoria and Prince Albert had one in 1840, and so did Consuelo Vanderbilt and the Duke of Marlborough in 1895.

The principal reason for the wedding reception was the obvious one—to provide a setting in which the newly married couple could receive, immediately after the ceremony, the congratulations and best wishes of family and friends. It could be a simple affair, or it could be quite lavish.

The breakfast wasn't really a breakfast at all. It was more like a luncheon, with more guests, more cold dishes, and cake. So long as it was held before one o'clock, however, the correct term for it was *breakfast.*

The format, from the 1870s and beyond, was similar, no matter where in America the wedding took place. Middle-class values were predominant and everyone wanted to emulate those whom they perceived to be "to the manner born." In the East it was especially important to look to the English to set the fashion. In the West, Victorians tried to emulate those in the East, particularly Boston and New York society.

Therefore, although some weddings were held in the late afternoon or evening, most followed the English custom of a noon ceremony, with a wedding breakfast thirty minutes afterward at the home of the bride. This allowed the couple time to leave on their wedding trip at a reasonable hour.

At a typical reception when the newly married couple arrived at the house, a musical ensemble concealed behind some palms played the Wedding March while they formed a receiving line.

Receiving the Guests

In addition to all the extravagant floral decorations throughout, a special area was created in one corner of a room for the bride and groom to receive their guests. It could be quite elaborate, such as a replica of a house made entirely of roses, large enough for the bride and groom to stand in, or as simple as a bower of tall ferns that framed the bridal pair. If the marriage ceremony had not been performed at home, the traditional white floral bell was suspended over the spot where they were to receive.

The parlor at The Hermitage in Ho-Ho-Kus, New Jersey, decorated for a wedding breakfast. The Hermitage, a lovely Gothic Revival house, has a parlor very much like those used in Victorian days for a home wedding. (Photograph by GF Studio/Rob Kern)

As a background for the bride and groom, flowers as exotic as orchids or as simple as wildflowers were sometimes hung on a screen. *Harper's Bazar* of October 31, 1885 went so far as to suggest making a tapestry of autumn leaves to hang behind the bride while she was receiving. This was to be created by her girl friends who would sew the leaves onto a piece of drugget (a floor cloth commonly placed under the dining room table to protect the rug).

Protocol for the receiving line called for the parents to be the first to congratulate the newly married couple, and then to stand nearby, but not in the line, to receive the guests. The maid of honor (or first bridesmaid as she was called in the early Victorian era) was the next to extend her best wishes after which she took her place next to the bride to assist her. At some weddings, the bridesmaids also stood in the receiving line, half at the right of the

The buffet table for the wedding breakfast was lavishly decorated and set with the family's finest silver and crystal. Since cutting the first slice of the wedding cake was the highlight of the reception, it usually had a place of honor. The centerpiece for this table at Adsmore is a silver basket with white flowers, flanked on either side with silver princess lamps. The yellow skirt and white cut-work embroidery tablecloth carry out the yellow and white color theme. (Photograph by Martin Studio, Princeton, Kentucky)

bride, and half at the left of the groom. The ushers did not stand with the bridal party because they had the responsibility to manage the line. Each usher in turn offered his right arm to a lady guest to conduct her to the married pair. Her gentleman escort followed. After the usher had presented the couple to the bride and groom, he then escorted them to the parents.

If a lady guest had no escort, the usher stayed with her until she had greeted the parents and then accompanied her to the breakfast room.

Etiquette required guests to address the bride first, unless they were acquainted with the groom and not the bride, in which case they were to congratulate the groom first and then have him introduce them to the bride. The correct form was to wish the bride joy, and to congratulate the groom. The bride was never congratulated because the implication was that she had conferred, rather than received, an honor when she married the man.

The bride stood in all her splendor throughout. She held her bouquet and did not remove her gloves. Gentlemen guests removed their hat and gloves when they entered the house for the reception; the ladies were to wear their bonnets.

The Breakfast

Some kind of a collation was expected by the guests once they had been through the receiving line. If the wedding was early in the morning, between eight and ten o'clock, and if it was small and informal, this could be as simple as tea, coffee, cakes, and claret with small tables set up around the room. Claret was an especially popular wine at middle-class weddings.

At a more elaborate breakfast following a late morning wedding, especially if there were as many as seventy-five guests, a long table would be set up in a separate room, or in the dining room up against the doors leading to the kitchen, with waiters standing ready to serve the guests "en buffet."

The decorations for this table could be quite lavish. Frequently, it was draped with lace or festoons of China silk with small bouquets of the bridal flower used to fasten the fabrics in place. Everything in the setting was planned to carry out the color scheme of the wedding— from the flowers to the icing on the cakes, the bonbons, the candles, and even the shades on the princess lamps. Only the wedding cake, if it was used as the centerpiece, was all white. This was traditional. This also was an occasion worthy of displaying all the family status symbols, so silver candelabra were placed at each end of the table and the family's finest silver, china, and glassware were used.

Guests at such a breakfast did not usually sit down, but were served standing. A gentleman brought refreshments from the table to the lady he had escorted to the wedding. In addition, waiters circulated with trays of delicately cut sandwiches (no crusts), finger rolls, buttered brown bread, and thin bread-and-butter sandwiches cut in fancy shapes. At some weddings, favors were worn by the waiters, for this was the practice in England.

The menu, or "perpendicular refreshments" as it was laughingly referred to, was more like a feast than a breakfast. Lobster Newburg was a particular favorite. So was jellied tongue. These two menus from 1891 and 1898 are typical for the late Victorian years.

Bouillon

Lobster Newburg   Salmon with Mayonnaise

Chicken Croquettes   Creamed Sweetbreads and Mushrooms

Sandwiches

Birds   Jellied Game   Salad

Individual Ices   Cake

Candied Fruit   Bonbons   Fruit   Coffee

Punch   Frappé   Champagne throughout

• 55 •

Food for a wedding breakfast is luncheon food. It was called a "breakfast" as long as it was held before one o'clock. A buffet is the best way to cope with modern food preferences and yet, it is authentically Victorian. (Photograph by G F Studio / Rob Kern)

Oysters
Boned Turkey Stuffed with Truffles and Mushrooms
Shrimp Salad served in Tomatoes
Tongue Sandwiches in Fancy Shapes

Olives   Salted Almonds   Bonbons
Ice Cream   Ices   Fancy Cakes   Fruits
Coffee

Although a bountiful table was expected, the more critical test was the perfection of the food served, both in taste and in presentation. The *Good Form* book on *Weddings* in 1891 stated unequivocally that "a very few well prepared, daintily served foods and drinks is much more satisfactory than a very elaborate one [menu] that fails in details."

Preserved fish, meats, and game were perfectly acceptable because by 1891 they were readily available everywhere. Hot bouillon and chocolate could be served in the winter, and iced tea, lemonade, and Apollinaris (a mineral water) in the summer. Wines, claret, champagne, or punch were perfectly appropriate if they were in accord with the family's "personal sense of fitness."

When Nellie Grant, the daughter of Ulysses S. Grant, was married in the White House in 1874, the President wanted a sumptuous affair, one that would be appropriate for the wedding of a daughter of the President of the United States. The menu consisted of soft-shelled crabs on toast, chicken croquettes with fresh peas, aspic of beef tongue, woodcock and snipe on toast, decorated broiled spring chicken, fresh strawberries with cream, Charlotte Russe, nesselrode pudding, and blanc mange. Even the distinguished guests were impressed.

If the wedding was to take place in the summer and the house was in the country, small round tables for the guests might be set up on the veranda or even on the lawn. No special entertainment was planned for the guests. Just being at the wedding was considered entertainment enough. Only at very lavish weddings, especially those in the evening, were there provisions for dancing. It was the exception rather than the rule.

Once the guests had extended their best wishes and had partaken of the refreshments, they were free to leave. There were no rules as to how long one must stay at a wedding.

When they had finished receiving their guests, the bride and groom led the way into the breakfast room, where only the members of the bridal party sat down for the wedding breakfast. The menu was the same as that for the guests, but it was served in courses. A second table could be set up nearby for the parents, the close relatives, and the clergyman who had performed the ceremony. Both tables were to be appropriately decorated.

During the breakfast, the bridesmaids and ushers would propose a toast to the bride and groom. They, of course, did not drink to their own toast, but immediately afterwards, proposed a toast in return to those at the table. When the bride and groom were being toasted, it was quite proper for the servants to participate in the toast.

Occasionally, a bride chose to have the wedding breakfast be a sit-down affair for all the guests. In this instance, the bride and groom led the way into the breakfast room, followed by the bride's father with the groom's mother. Next came the groom's father with the bride's

Punch, being one of the beverages offered at a Victorian wedding, may be either alcoholic or nonalcoholic, depending on the preference of the family. (Photograph by GF Studio / Rob Kern)

mother. The bridal party then followed led by the best man and the first bridesmaid, and then the ushers and bridesmaids in pairs.

At this type of occasion, the father of the groom proposed a toast to the health of the bride and groom, and the father of the bride responded. Then, the groom proposed a toast to the health of the bridesmaids, and the best man returned this toast.

The Wedding Cake

A typical Victorian wedding had not one cake, but three. There was the wedding cake itself, which gradually evolved from the ornately decorated towering cake of the early Victorian era to a less imposing but still beautifully decorated cake of the later years. Then there were the bride's cake and the groom's cake. Custom seems to have varied as to which cakes were given to the guests, although the form in which they received it was the same. It was cut and boxed and given to the guests as they left the reception. Sometimes these boxes of cake were also sent to those who could not come to the wedding.

One custom that some Victorians borrowed from the past was that of threading narrow strips of wedding cake through the wedding ring to give as favors. Originally, the small pieces of cake were to be threaded through the bride's ring on the day of the wedding (nine times was considered lucky), but in practice, the bridesmaids cut the pieces and threaded them through the wedding ring the day before. (Victorians were superstitious and believed it was bad luck to remove the wedding ring from the finger once it had been put there during the marriage ceremony.) These little pieces of cake were wrapped in pretty paper, tied with ribbons, and distributed to the young unmarried ladies and gentlemen at the wedding breakfast, who wanted to believe that by placing the piece of cake under their pillows that night they would dream of their future husband or wife.

The wedding cake was traditionally a dark, rich fruit-cake, with an ornate white frosting of scrolls, orange blossoms, and other delicate decorations. This cake was on display at the wedding, but it was not consumed. As a highlight of the reception, the bride was to cut the first piece, with the groom standing at her side, a symbol of

Our tiered wedding cake at The Hermitage was made for us by Susan Lang Simon. (Photograph by GF Studio / Rob Kern)

her first domestic task. The cake itself was then carefully sealed and stored until their twenty-fifth anniversary.

A second batch of the same cake was baked in flat tins, to be cut up and placed in small cake boxes lined with lace paper for the guests to take home. These boxes, which were usually five by two inches in size, ranged from plain white tied with a white satin ribbon to those covered with white satin embroidered with orange blossoms, to sterling-silver boxes engraved with the initials of the bride and groom formed into a monogram. Even the satin ribbon used to tie the boxes could be decorated.

Allisandro Filippini, the chef at Delmonico's restaurant in New York, which was the dernier cri for social events in the late Victorian era, used this recipe for his wedding cakes.

Wedding Cake. Place in a large bowl one pound of powdered sugar and one pound of well-washed butter. Grate in the rind of two lemons; and with the hand knead well for ten minutes. Break in ten whole eggs, two at a time, and knead for ten minutes longer. Mix in a plate a teaspoonful of ground cinnamon, a teaspoonful of ground cloves, two of ground allspice, one of mace, and one of grated nutmeg, and add these, with half a gill of confectioners' molasses. Mix well for one minute with the hand. Add one pound of well-sifted flour, stirring for two minutes more. Add two pounds of currants, two pounds of Sultana raisins, two pounds of Malaga raisins, one pound of candied citron, finely sliced, one gill of Jamaica rum, and one gill of brandy. Mix the whole well together for fifteen minutes—using both hands, if necessary. Butter the interior of a plain, five-quart, round cake-mold. Line the bottom and sides with paper, leaving it an inch and a half higher than the edge of the mold. Pour in all the preparation, and place it in a very slow oven to bake for five hours. Unmold, detach the paper, and turn the cake bottom up on a wire pastry-grate. After

*The cake made for the wedding on July 6, 1893 of the Duke and Duchess of York, who later became King George V and Queen Mary of England, was created by the Queen's Baker at Windsor Castle. (*Illustrated London News, *July 15, 1893)*

As the guests left the reception, each took a small box of wedding cake. Sometimes these elegant boxes of cake were sent to those who could not attend. (Photograph by Martin Studio, Princeton, Kentucky)

The wedding cake at Adsmore has a lovely basket of flowers on the top that would have been saved.

The wedding cake was not necessarily baked at home. It could be ordered from a baker or even a store.

The bride's cake and the groom's cake were less elaborate than the wedding cake, although they, too, were decorated appropriately for the wedding. Occasionally, a creative baker might bake them in the shape of two hearts placed side by side on a tray, but the traditional way was to have two small round cakes placed at either end of a table. Hers was a white cake, his was a dark one. At the breakfast for the bridal party both cakes were cut into as many pieces as there were groomsmen and bridesmaids.

Baked in the bride's cake were a coin, a thimble, a ring, and a button, each a symbol for what the recipient might expect in the future.

> The ring for marriage within a year;
> The penny for wealth, my dear;
> The thimble for an old maid or bachelor born;
> The button for sweethearts all forlorn.

The bridesmaid who found the ring in her piece of cake was the envy of all, because tradition ruled that she would be the next bride.

ten minutes, glaze it with one egg-white that has been beaten in a bowl with four ounces of extra-fine sugar, using the spatula; use a knife to apply the glazing. Now lay the cake in a warm place to dry for two hours. Then beat up the white of an egg with four ounces of extra-fine sugar for ten minutes, and glaze the cake as before, evenly all around, and lay aside for two hours more. After it is thoroughly dried, lay it on a round wooden board, covered with a fancy paper that is two inches wider than the board. Procure a fancy wedding-bell, with a miniature bride and groom standing under, lay it in the centre of the cake, fastening it on with glacé royale, by pressing the glacé royale through a paper cornet with a fancy tube. Decorate the surface of the cake with ornaments made of the glacé; also a fancy border around the edge and base. Let it dry slightly for two hours, and it is ready for use.

Glacé royale. Put into a small bowl half of the white of a raw egg and two ounces of extra-fine sugar, and beat well with a spatula. Drop in carefully just one drop, and no more, of lemon juice; beat again for five minutes until thickened; it will be ready for use.

Bride's going-away costume

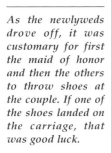

As the newlyweds drove off, it was customary for first the maid of honor and then the others to throw shoes at the couple. If one of the shoes landed on the carriage, that was good luck.

The maid of honor chose the first piece, and then the bridesmaids selected theirs in alphabetical order. Toward the end of the Victorian era, some of the bridesmaids lost interest in looking for the ring in the cake, because they didn't want to soil their gloves.

The bride's cake itself was important because symbolically it represented the ambrosia of matrimony. As an alternative, the bride could serve small sugared white cakes from a silver salver, one of which would have the ring baked in it.

Leaving for the Wedding Trip

Once the cakes were cut, the bride and groom disappeared to their respective dressing rooms to change into their traveling clothes. Generally, the bride's most intimate friends, including the bridesmaids, went with her. It was here that a bride might give each of the group a flower from her bouquet.

When the bride was ready to leave, she was met at the foot of the stairs by the groom dressed in his suit of checked or striped cheviot, and carrying a hat and gloves. The bride was advised not to wear a gown that was conspicuously new out of respect to the sensitivity of her husband, who might not want people to know that he was just married.

At this point only the family and the most intimate of friends were left at the reception. They all kissed the bride goodbye as she and the groom walked to the carriage that he had provided to drive them to their destination. The horses were decorated with wedding favors, and the coachman and footman wore huge white bouquets on their coats. In England, the wedding carriage would have been drawn by four white horses.

As they drove off, the newlyweds were showered with rice and satin slippers. The maid of honor was to throw the first slipper. If one slipper landed on the carriage, it was considered good luck forever, and if it was the left slipper, it was even better luck.

Meanwhile, the best man had preceded the bride and groom to the train or the steamer to look after their luggage and to see them off. No one asked where they were going. That was considered bad taste. Only the best man knew, and he was sworn to secrecy.

Early Victorian Wedding Celebrations

Although the formal wedding breakfast is the most typical Victorian reception, it was by no means the only way to celebrate a marriage. In the early days of the era, up to the early 1860s, regional customs prevailed.

For example, in the South, wedding receptions were quite often held in the ballroom of the plantation, after six o'clock in the evening, preferably before the month of June, because it was cooler then. Many of the guests were friends and relatives who were staying there for the duration of the festivities. The party could last for hours. Music was provided by ladies of the family who took turns playing the piano and the harp, and everyone danced into the wee hours of the night, fortified by a potent artillery punch. The bride and groom had no formal sendoff. They left quietly sometime during the festivities to go by coach to their honeymoon destination.

In the West, especially in the rural areas, a wedding was one of the few occasions when everyone could temporarily put aside the hard work of building a frontier to have fun. The celebration usually lasted for days, both before and after the ceremony, with alternate hours of feasting and dancing into the early hours of the morning.

The food was hearty. It might be prepared by the bride and her friends or by a local tavern. In 1840, the Wilcox Log Tavern in Waupun, Wisconsin, offered this menu for a wedding feast:

> A big gobbler, fattened for the occasion . . . a bowl of pickled cabbage, a dish of baked beans, a plate of boiled beets fantastically decorated with cloves, and after that the crowning dish of all—a glorious jelly cake, well seasoned with ginger, and molasses plentifully spread between the layers of jelly.

The wedding cake was created by friends of the bride. Each one baked a single layer of her best cake recipe and brought it to the wedding. These layers, all different, were stacked one on top of the other, with jelly or applesauce as a filling in between, since white sugar for frosting was scarce. Thus was formed a Friendship Cake that became the centerpiece for the wedding feast. If a bride had many friends, there might be more than one stack cake on the table.

One tradition that was extremely popular was the shivaree. After the newlyweds had gone to their house and were presumably settled in, a crowd gathered in front with all kinds of noisemakers—pots and pans, shotguns, bells, and pistols—making a din until the newlyweds acknowledged their presence. The crowd continued their noisemaking until invited in for refreshments. This activity was not necessarily approved by everyone. A book of manners published in 1850 considered it "inconsistent with our present ideas of refinement."

One of the customs that did prevail in the West in the 1840s and 1850s was the announcement of marriages in the newspapers. How it was announced and where it was placed in the paper depended on whether or not the bride and groom sent the editor a piece of their wedding cake and a gold dollar. A typical one from 1856 states:

• 61 •

MARRIED

On the 26 ult. by Reverend J. W. Terrill, Mr. Peter S. Baker of Johnson county and Miss Sara M. Harvey of Howard county.

The above couple is bound to be happy, for they started right, the groom sending a gold dollar, and the bride a portion of the cake along with their notice of the marriage. Good luck, health, and happiness attend them, and may they live many years to greet the return of the day that made them one flesh.

If the editor was especially generous, he even added a poem to the announcement as a special felicitation to the couple. This one was printed in the Glasgow (Kentucky) *Weekly Times* on October 12, 1854.

> May breezes blow gently,
>   And sweet flowers bloom
> O'er their pathway through life
>   To the cold silent tomb.
> And free from all sorrow,
>   As angels above,
> May their life be all smiles,
>   Bright sunshine and love.

If the couple did not pay the expected tariff, a brief notice was printed in some out-of-the-way corner of the paper. This practice prevailed until the 1860s.

As part of the ritual of the wedding breakfast, guests looked forward to admiring the gifts received by the bride. These were usually displayed in a room on the second floor of the house. This exquisite linen tea cloth with a deep border of point de Venise lace and twelve matching napkins was received as a gift by a bride in Cleveland, Ohio, in 1880. Another handsome gift was the beautifully painted porcelain tea service. (Photograph by Scott Bowron)

Silver wedding gifts were considered quite "proper," and the more elegant, the better. A fish slice was a practical gift that could also be quite elaborate— a status symbol for those who wished to impress other guests with the value of the gift they had presented to the bride. This example of around 1880 is hand-engraved gilded sterling with a mother-of-pearl handle featuring the bride's maiden initial. (Photograph by Scott Bowron)

Displaying the Wedding Presents

Whether or not to display the wedding presents at the reception was an issue that was debated often, especially during the late Victorian era. Gifts were sent to the bride as soon as the wedding invitation was received and could be delivered by a servant or sent directly by the store where they had been purchased. Although presents were intended as tokens of esteem and love by those who wished the bride well, they also became symbols of status and displays of wealth.

Traditionally, admiring the presents had been part of the ritual of the Victorian wedding. They were arranged in a room separate from the activities of the reception, usually on the second floor of the house. Each one was identified with the card of the donor. Some brides did their best to make the display an attractive one, using a dark velvet cloth on which to place some of the presents, surrounding each with a wreath of flowers. Those that were too large for such a display, such as furniture or even a piano (this was not unusual in the late Victorian era) were acknowledged with a card.

If the wedding reception was at a hotel instead of at home, the presents were taken there to be displayed. When Maud Sambourne, daughter of Mr. and Mrs. Linley Sambourne of London, was married in 1898, her presents were displayed in one of the rooms at the Royal Palace Hotel, where refreshments were served after the wedding.

The quantity and value of the gifts received were evidently an important measure of the esteem in which the bride and groom were held. Newspaper accounts quite often mentioned this, as the one in 1892 for the wedding of Mamye Smith and R.D. Garrett, which noted: "One of the evidences of the high regard these young people are held in is the costly and numerous presents they received. These possibly surpassed in number and value than ever before given to a bride in Princeton [Kentucky]."

In 1886, the gifts received by Ella Sturgis for her wedding in Wisconsin were noted: "The presents were numerous and very valuable, consisting of jewels, gold and silverware, articles of crystal, china, bronze, and many other things fitted for household use and adornment. They were displayed on long crimson tables in the library." The newspaper account then went on to list the gifts and the donor of each. The father and mother of the groom gave a very large and complete case of spoons, knives, forks of every size and description, also a handsome set of china. The father and mother of the bride gave a large solid-silver pitcher and goblets. The list went on for a full column.

When Robert L. Gault married Mary L. Jones in Westport, Connecticut, on December 21, 1881, the *Westporter* listed more than sixty gifts ranging from a lace tidy, a set of plated forks, a roll of carpet, a black-walnut bracket with a curtain of painted satin and elegant fringe to a fancy reception chair upholstered in raw silk and plush from members of the Compo Engine Company and an ivoryware tea set of seventy pieces from the teachers of the Memorial Church Sunday School.

That same paper, a few months earlier on September 24th, reprinted an article from the *Cincinnati Saturday Night* about the practice at some society weddings of using detectives to guard the presents.

DETECTIVES AT WEDDINGS

In the East detectives are employed to attend big weddings. It is their business to hover around the collection of costly presents and see that none of the high-toned guests steal anything. It is only at weddings attended by the very highest toned that detectives are necessary, which is rather a compliment to people who don't pretend to any particular tone themselves. These detectives have to be men of intelligence and good address, and they are required to attire themselves in swallow-tails of the regulation pattern, so that they may pass for guests and excite no remark while exercising the necessary vigilance . . . Kleptomania, unknown to the lower walks of life, where they simply steal when they take something that doesn't belong to them, is an unfortunate malady that sometimes attacks people moving in the higher circles, and it is to guard against this that detectives are engaged for these great events which dazzle the social world.

Most brides didn't go this far. They asked a trusted friend to stay in the room with the presents during the reception.

Those who influenced social law gradually expressed concern regarding the undue emphasis on quantity and value and recommended that the entire practice of displaying the wedding presents at the reception be eliminated. Instead, they suggested that the bride give a tea for her most intimate friends a day or two before the wedding so that they could admire them.

Some brides, however, continued to display their presents without the donor cards, as a concession to the criticism that they were becoming ostentatious. Others preferred to continue the tradition of displaying the presents with the donor card at the reception. It became an individual decision that carried well over into the next century.

Anniversaries of Weddings

A romantic event such as the anniversary of a wedding was especially appealing to the sentimental Victorians. Regardless of the years, they celebrated by gathering as many of the original members of the wedding party who could attend to re-enact the events of that great moment when they became man and wife.

Guests arriving for the anniversary party were greeted by the bride and groom standing under a marriage bell, with their bridesmaids at their side. Ideally, they would all be wearing the costumes they wore on the day of the wedding. Those who were sentimental let out the seams of the wedding gown or the bridesmaids' gowns if the years had added some weight to their bones. Being dressed in the original attire was part of the romance of the occasion. Those who were pragmatic had a new gown for the occasion. All carried bouquets, just as they had on the day of the wedding.

All wedding anniversaries were not equal. Some, like the twenty-fifth and the fiftieth, were important milestones; others, like the first, second, third, fifth, and the fifteenth, were more or less routine. The tenth was significant because it marked the approach of middle age, a time when the husband and wife could relax and have some fun; the twentieth was not even alluded to by those Victorians who were superstitious because there was a Scotch belief that one or the other of the couple would die within the year if this anniversary was celebrated.

Themes for Each Wedding Anniversary

Each anniversary was given a distinguishing name that implied the theme for the celebration as well as the gifts that would be appropriate. This theme was carried out in the most minute detail, including the invitations, the decorations in the home, the ornaments on the table, and even the serving pieces for the refreshments.

Cotton Wedding	First Year
Paper Wedding	Second Year
Leather Wedding	Third Year
Wooden Wedding	Fifth Year
Woolen Wedding	Seventh Year
Tin Wedding	Tenth Year
Silk and Linen Wedding	Twelfth Year
Crystal Wedding	Fifteenth Year
China Wedding	Twentieth Year
(superstitious Victorians celebrated this on the twenty-first year)	
Silver Wedding	Twenty-fifth Year
Pearl Wedding	Thirtieth Year
Ruby Wedding	Fortieth Year
Golden Wedding	Fiftieth Year
Diamond Wedding	Sixtieth Year
(some believed this should be for the Seventy-fifth year)	

The longer a marriage was successful, the more precious the recognition.

Invitations designated the year of the marriage and the date of the anniversary.

Mr. and Mrs. Charles Smith
At Home
Tuesday afternoon, December the third
from four until seven o'clock

1897–1898   181 Joy Street

The Tin Wedding

The tin wedding anniversary, which occurred after ten years of marriage, was a signal for general frolic. The marriage had matured, they were comfortable with one another and the couple could enjoy a good joke, even when it was targeted at them. It was a fun anniversary. Friends commissioned local tinsmiths to create humorous gifts that were intended to make fun of some of the characteristics of the couple. As each one was opened at the celebration, it became part of the entertainment.

Many of these pieces have been collected over the years as examples of folk art. Although they hold their own secrets as to why they were originally created, viewed with a sense of history and some imagination they provide an interesting glimpse into the sense of humor of the Victorians: a tin cradle could have teased a couple for having a large family; a giant tin pocketwatch on an equally oversized chain could have symbolized the tendency of a couple to be always late; a tin top hat and fancy tin bonnet might have been intended for a couple with a quiet social life; an oversized comb could signify the need for a tool to work out "marriage snarls"; a pair of tin slippers could have been made for two happy souls. The possibilities were limited only by the imagination of the giver and the skill of the tinsmith.

Not all tin gifts were intended to be humorous. Some, like kitchen utensils, were practical. Others were decorative. Baskets made of woven tin, compotes decorated with tin curls to hold fruit, tin candlesticks, tin cake covers with beaded edges were just some of the items that a talented tinsmith could create. One father-in-law gave his "tin" to the "bride" in the form of a handsome check placed inside a tin pocketbook.

The Silver Wedding

The silver wedding anniversary was an important milestone. Although the couple were now middle-aged, they were in the prime of life, at a point where they could stop to count their blessings. The celebration rituals reflected this.

Invitation cards were printed in silver, with the dates of the wedding and the anniversary as well as the name of the husband and the name of the lady as she was known before the marriage.

• 65 •

A tenth-anniversary tin compote with a collection of velvet fruit and vegetables. From the Barry Cohen Collection, courtesy America Hurrah Antiques and David A. Schorsch, Inc., New York City.

Silver Wedding
* 1870–1895 *
Rev. J. J. Hall, D. D. and Wife,
cordially invite you to be present at their
Twenty-fifth Wedding Anniversary
to take place at the
Pastorium
136 Park Avenue, Norfolk, Virginia
Tuesday Evening, July 16th, 1895,
Receive from 8 till 11 P. M.

Showing its age, yet with the silver printing and edging around the card still elegant, the Silver Wedding invitation of the Rev. J.J. Hall, D.D. and Wife, 1875. (Courtesy Hunter House Victorian Museum, Norfolk, Virginia)

Some couples went so far as to transcribe the original marriage notice from the newspaper to include with the invitation.

In the later years of the Victorian era, when sensible reform was being urged to counteract the escalating expectations for gifts at weddings and anniversaries, these invitations were also quite often engraved with the words "No presents received."

In order to have a perfect re-enactment of their wedding day, the silver-anniversary celebration was to be scheduled at exactly the hour at which the original marriage took place. The "bridal pair," dressed in their original wedding garments, formed a receiving line along with their bridesmaids and groomsmen, all caught up in the sentimental mood of the moment.

If it had been a morning wedding, and this hour was not practical for the anniversary, then it could be ignored and the party planned for the evening. And if the wedding garments no longer fit, the bride could have a second wedding dress, any color but white or black. Silver-gray trimmed with steel and lace was considered a fashionable approach to carry out the theme of a silver wedding.

Whether or not the marriage ceremony should be repeated at the party was a decision left up to the couple. Although this was considered appropriate for any anniversary of a wedding, it was especially favored for the twenty-fifth and the fiftieth. *Decorum* had a definite point of view on this matter:

The earlier anniversaries are rather too trivial occasions upon which to introduce this ceremony, especially since the parties may not yet have had sufficient time to discover whether an application for divorce may not yet be deemed necessary by one or the other. But there is a certain impressiveness in seeing a husband and wife who have remained faithful to each other for a quarter or half a century publicly renewing their vows of fidelity and love, which then can only mean "till death do us part."

Ideally, the clergyman who performed the ceremony originally, presided again.

President Rutherford B. Hayes and his wife Lucy chose to repeat their vows at a celebration of their twenty-fifth anniversary which was held in the White House on December 30, 1877. Mrs. Hayes wore her original flowered-satin wedding dress, let out at the seams to accommodate the changes in her figure. Friends and participants who attended the original wedding were there to witness the Rev. Dr. L.D. Cabe of Delaware, Ohio, perform again the ceremony that he originally conducted at their wedding in 1852. Even the little niece, now a young lady, who had held the bride's hand during the original ceremony now stood with Lucy Hayes again, holding her hand. It was the kind of moment that was worthy of a lace handkerchief to wipe away the tears of sentiment.

The entertainment at this and all other anniversaries inevitably included a bride's cake with the gold ring baked inside for some fortunate guest to claim. The bride cut the cake, just as she had twenty-five years earlier, after which refreshments were served from the bountiful buffet, toasts were drunk, and speeches made. It was not uncommon also to have sentimental poems and songs dedicated to the bride and groom.

Some husbands, caught up in the sentiment of the anniversary, gave their wives a second wedding ring.

As when, amid the rites divine,
I took thy troth, and plighted mine
To thee, sweet wife, my second ring
A token and a pledge I bring.
This ring shall wed, till death us part,
Thy riper virtues to my heart—
Those virtues which, before untried,
The wife has added to the bride.

When anniversary celebrations first became popular around the 1870s, presents to commemorate the year conformed rigidly to the theme. For the earlier ones, this was a relatively inexpensive remembrance. By the time the twenty-fifth anniversary came along, however, a suitable gift of silver could cost as much as $50. Custom called for these to be engraved with the words "Silver Wedding," and the initials of the pair engraved in a true lover's knot, or a sentimental motto. Gifts that were appropriate included clocks, bracelets, ornaments to hang from a chatelaine, picture frames, hand-mirrors set in fretted silver, silver parasol handles, pitchers, vases, silver vegetable dishes, and even silver soup tureens.

As time went on, the giving of gifts became a matter of ostentation and gradually, especially for the silver wedding, it became good custom to add "No presents received" to the invitation. The prevailing attitude was that a couple who had reached their silver wedding were beyond the need of appealing to the generosity of their friends.

In addition to the celebration with friends, some couples also repeated their wedding journey. In the 1890s there was a little route in England called the "silver wedding journey."

The Golden Wedding

Because not many people reached the age to celebrate it, the golden-wedding anniversary was considered impressive. Invitations were printed in gold on thick white paper, and as many of those who participated in the original wedding were gathered together with the happy couple. If they still fit after fifty years, the original wedding garments were worn.

Renewing the marriage vows was definitely in order. In fact, it was almost poetic—a couple in the twilight of their lives promising, once again, to love and to cherish. They were to stand under a great marriage bell, made of fully ripe wheat, sheaves of corn, and roses of a pure gold color, and the bride would carry a bouquet, just as she had done fifty years ago.

This celebration, like all the others, called for a bride's cake with a ring baked in it, but it was to be more lavishly decorated, possibly with a monogram of their initials and the date of the wedding.

One golden anniversary that was widely acclaimed was that of the Rev. Dr. and Mrs. Ray Palmer, which was

celebrated on October 11, 1882 in Newark, New Jersey. It was described in the January 1883 *Sunday Magazine* as one of the most enjoyable events in Newark society. He was a famous hymnologist whose best-known hymn had the lines that are still familiar today:

> My faith looks up to thee
> Thou lamb of Calvary.

At seven o'clock a wedding party was formed, preceded by Dr. Pennington who had been a groomsman at their wedding. The bridal pair of fifty years marched into the parlor and took their position under the marriage bell. It was made of goldenrod with streamers of roses and pines. There they repeated their vows in the presence of friends and family.

Afterwards, one minister congratulated the couple; another presented them with a scrapbook bound in Russian leather containing 120 letters from friends, including Harriet Beecher Stowe and John G. Whittier. The letter from Oliver Wendell Holmes is especially eloquent:

> Beverly Farms, Massachusetts
> September 30, 1882

My Dear Mr. Palmer:
    Your old friend and Andover fellow-student sends you his cordial and affectionate greeting on this golden anniversary of your wedded life.
    May that life flow on in tranquil and happy companionship with the partner of all its vicissitudes until heaven calls you from singing hymns of earth to join in the songs of angels.

> Always faithfully yours,
> Oliver Wendell Holmes

Because it was a rare anniversary, the Golden Wedding appealed to the sentimental heartstrings of many Victorians, whether or not they had yet reached this milestone. It was a romantic dream that they hoped to achieve.

Three Notable Weddings

VICTORIA and ALBERT
The First Victorian Wedding

On the tenth of October in 1839, when her cousin Albert of Saxe-Coburg and Gotha and his brother Ernest came for a visit that Queen Victoria had tried to forestall, little did she know that it was to become the turning point in her life.

The marriage of Victoria and Albert had been orchestrated for a long time by their uncle, King Leopold of the Belgians. She knew it and he knew it. But as she entered the second year of her reign she began to have doubts, first about the need to be married so soon, and then about Albert as the man she wanted to marry.

To Lord Melbourne, her mentor, Victoria expressed her concern that she was so accustomed to having her own way, it was ten to one that she couldn't agree with anybody.

To her Uncle Leopold, who was patiently forging his plan, she tried to forestall a visit from her cousin Albert by writing:

> Though all the reports of Albert are most favourable, and though I have little doubt I shall like him, still one can never answer beforehand for feelings, and I may not have the feeling for him which is requisite to ensure happiness. I may like him as a friend, and as a cousin, and as a brother, but not more; and should this be the case (which is not likely), I am very anxious that it should be understood that I am not guilty of any breach of promise, for I never gave any. I am sure you will understand my anxiety, for I should otherwise, were this not completely understood, be in a very painful position. As it is, I am rather nervous about the visit, for the subject I allude to is not an agreeable one to me.

Her uncle persisted, however, and on the 10th of October in 1839, Albert and his brother Ernest arrived. The strong-minded young queen was overwhelmed by the handsome Albert, whom she described in her journal that night as "beautiful…such beautiful blue eyes, and exquisite nose and such a pretty mouth with delicate mustachios and slight, but very slight, whiskers; a beautiful figure, broad in the shoulders and a fine waist."

She was fascinated by him, and little by little over the next few days, realized that the "feeling" she was determined to have, had, indeed, become a reality.

By October 14, Victoria had made up her mind to marry Albert and on the 15th of October she recorded her proposal to him in her journal:

15 October 1839

> At about ½ p. 12 I sent for Albert; he came to the Closet where I was alone, and after a few minutes I said to him, that I thought he must be aware why I wished [him] to come here, and that it would make me too happy if he would consent to what I wished (to marry me); we embraced each other over and over again, and he was so kind, so affectionate; Oh! to feel I was, and am, loved by such an Angel as Albert was too great delight to describe! he is perfection; perfection in every way—in beauty—in everything!

Albert was both thrilled and relieved. He had been waiting in the wings for a long time.

The engagement was kept secret for one month during which they had time to get to know one another better and to make plans for the wedding. Some of the excerpts from her journal during this period reflect the first blush of romance that was to grow into the most famous love story of the era.

19 October 1839

My dearest Albert came to me at 10 m. to 12 and stayed with me till 20 m. p. 1. Such a pleasant happy time. He looked over my shoulder and watched me writing to the Duchess of Northumberland, and to the Duchess of Sutherland; and he scraped out some mistakes I had made. I told him I felt so grateful to him and would do everything to make him happy. I gave him a ring with the date of the ever dear to me 15th engraved in it.

He gave her a heavy gold serpent ring, the symbol of longevity, as well as a bracelet with a miniature . . . of him in uniform. This became one of her favorite pieces of jewelry and is seen in many of her portraits.

27 October 1839

I signed some papers and warrants etc. and he was so kind as to dry them with blotting paper for me. We talked a good deal together, and he clasped me so tenderly in his arms, and kissed me again and again . . . and was so affectionate, so full of love! Oh! what happiness is this! How I do adore him!! I kissed his dear hand. He embraced me again so tenderly.

1 November 1839

At 7 m. p. 6 came my most beloved Albert and stayed with me till 10 m. p. 7 . . . He was so affectionate, so kind, so dear, we kissed each other again and again . . . Oh! what too sweet delightful moments are these! Oh! how blessed, how happy I am to think he is really mine; I can scarcely believe myself so blessed. I kissed his dear hand, and do feel so grateful to him; he is such an angel, such a very great angel!—We sit so nicely side by side on that little blue sofa; no two Lovers could ever be happier than we are!

During this time, they both agreed on the 10th of February 1840 as the date for the wedding. Now that she had made up her mind, she wanted to have the wedding take place as early as possible, and he believed that was best because "the relations between a betrothed pair when the fact is public property may often appear indelicate."

On November 10 the Queen announced her decision to her mother and to the Privy Council. They, in turn, requested that she make it public, so on November 23, 1839, the *London Gazette* printed her marriage declaration for all her subjects to see.

I have caused you to be summoned at the present time, in order that I may acquaint you with my resolution in a matter which deeply concerns the welfare of my people, and the happiness of my future life.

It is my intention to ally myself in marriage with the Prince Albert of Saxe-Coburg and Gotha. Deeply impressed with the solemnity of the engagement which I am about to contract, I have not come to this decision without mature consideration, not without feeling a strong assurance that, with the blessing of Almighty God, it will at once secure my domestic felicity and serve the interests of my country.

I have thought fit to make this resolution known to you at the earliest period, in order that you may be fully apprised of a matter so highly important to me and to my kingdom, and which I persuade myself will be most acceptable to all my loving subjects.

The wedding was scheduled for one o'clock in the Chapel Royal of St. James's Palace. The day was cold, wet, and windy, but it didn't deter the crowds from lining the route of the procession that left Buckingham Palace at 12:30 for the short trip to St. James's.

Victoria was radiant, as a bride should be, and as the queen she had made every effort to ensure that her wedding costume was made of materials manufactured in Great Britain. The dress was made of white Spitalfields satin and Honiton lace, made in the village of Beer. Some have described it as a "tasteless muddle." It was simple compared to royal wedding dresses of the past, made of yards of white satin, with a deep flounce of Honiton lace, a low-cut neckline and puffed sleeves, covered with bows and orange blossoms. With its eighteen-foot train, it overwhelmed her 4'11" frame.

A coronet of orange blossoms held her veil. Even though she was a queen, the symbolism of the orange blossoms for the bride was too significant to ignore.

Her twelve train bearers were dressed in white tulle

dresses that Victoria herself had designed, and on their heads they wore short white veils with a wreath of white roses set straight on top. They had to huddle together as they moved down the aisle because the train was too short for all twelve of them to be spaced at a comfortable distance.

Perhaps because she was a queen, her jewelry was a major part of Victoria's adornment. She wore the Order and Star of the Garter, her Turkish diamond necklace and earrings, and the brooch that Albert had given her as a wedding gift, a large sapphire surrounded by diamonds.

Her mother, the Duchess of Kent, wore a dress of white and silver, with a diamond tiara and feathers on her head, and a train of blue velvet. All other guests had been requested not to wear feathers as they would interfere with the view of the passing scene. They were, however, encouraged to make and wear wedding favors of lace and ribbon trimmed with sprigs of orange blossoms.

Promptly at one o'clock there was a flourish of trumpets and the procession began. Albert approached the altar first to the strains of Handel's "See the Conquering Hero Come." He was dressed in the uniform of a British field marshal. The scarlet tunic and white knee breeches were set off by a long tasseled sash, and on each shoulder he wore the customary bridal favor, a white satin bow. The diamond Star and Badge of the Most Noble Order of the Garter, which Victoria had presented to him as a wedding gift, was draped across his chest. As he stood there, a green velvet Bible in his hand, he was every inch the handsome prince of Victoria's dreams.

After his procession had moved into the Chapel, Victoria's was formed in the throne room. Lord Melbourne, bearing the Sword of State, flanked on either side by a Captain of the Yeomen of the Guard, walked immediately before the Queen, who was escorted by her uncle, the Duke of Sussex. As she entered the Chapel, the flourish of trumpets ceased and the organ began to play.

Victoria and Albert had read the marriage service together the night before and had practiced how to manage the ring. She had requested that the word "obey" be kept in the ceremony, because although as queen she could not take an oath to obey, as a wife she could.

Her impressions of the actual service were recorded in her journal:

The Ceremony was very imposing, and fine and simple, and I think ought to make an everlasting impression on every one who promises at the Altar to keep what he or she promises. Dearest Albert repeated everything very distinctly. I felt so happy when the ring was put on, and by Albert.

She promised to love, honor, and obey and he promised to love and cherish her. It was a touching moment that brought tears, not only to the eyes of Victoria, but to all who witnessed it.

After the ceremony, the bride and groom retired to the gold throne room to sign the marriage register. On the way, Victoria kissed her aunt, the Dowager Queen Adelaide, but only shook hands with her mother, reasserting her position that since becoming the queen she could no longer be dominated by her. This did not go unnoticed.

Before they left St. James's Palace, an attendant gave the queen a cloth bag that held her gift for each of the bridesmaids, which was a turquoise eagle based on Albert's crest, with a ruby beak and pearl claws, enclosed in a dark blue velvet case. In addition, gold remembrance rings, designed especially as a souvenir of the wedding, were given to seventy of the most important guests. Each ring had the queen's portrait carved in gold.

After they had signed the register, Victoria and Albert returned alone to Buckingham Palace, where they spent a quiet half hour together before joining the guests at the wedding breakfast. The highlight of the festivities was the cutting of the elaborate wedding cake by the bride and the groom.

Weighing three hundred pounds, the cake was nine feet in circumference and sixteen inches deep. Topping it was a figure of Britannia blessing figures of the bride and groom. These figures were twelve inches tall. At the feet of the prince was the effigy of a dog, symbol of fidelity, and at the feet of the queen, two turtledoves symbolizing the felicities of the marriage state. A cupid held an open volume with the day and the date of the marriage.

The wedding breakfast did not last too long. The bride and groom left at 4 P.M. for the three-hour drive to Windsor Castle where they were to spend a four-day honeymoon.

Her going-away outfit was a white silk gown trimmed with swansdown, and a bonnet with orange blossoms. This all white traveling costume was to influence what brides wore for their going-away outfits for many years to come.

That night she wrote in her journal: "Oh, this was the happiest day of my life." The romantic Victorian era had begun.

CONSUELO VANDERBILT and
THE DUKE OF MARLBOROUGH
One of the Most Notable Weddings of the Victorian Era

The Vanderbilt-Marlborough wedding that took place in New York City on November 6, 1895 was one of the most notable weddings of the Victorian era. Both *Harper's Weekly* and *The New York Times* described it as "unequaled in magnificence by any wedding this country has seen." It excited a great deal of interest. The young American woman who entered the church as Consuelo Vanderbilt would emerge as the Duchess of Marlborough. What could be more romantic?

Crowds of onlookers gathered early, both in front of the Vanderbilt mansion at Madison Avenue and 72nd Street and at St. Thomas's Church on Fifth Avenue. It took more than two hundred policemen to manage the businessmen, laborers, clubmen, nurses with baby carriages, fashionable women and not so fashionable women—all craning their necks to catch a glimpse of the wedding party.

Although the Vanderbilts worshipped at St. Bartholomew's Church on Park Avenue, St. Thomas's was chosen for the ceremony, because a larger church was needed to accommodate the fortunate recipients of the 3000 invitations sent out. It was no secret that this was a marriage arranged by Alva Vanderbilt, mother of Consuelo, who had groomed her daughter from early childhood to make an illustrious match. She had been tutored at home in English, French, and German, and drilled in proper deportment. Like many Victorian children, she had been made to sit and walk with a metal rod strapped to her back at her waist and her head to encourage an aristocratic bearing.

Everyone also knew that Alva, who was ostracized by society after her divorce from Consuelo's father, Willie, had not invited "a single person bearing the name of Vanderbilt" to the wedding, except the bride's two brothers, and the bride's father, who was to be tolerated because he was to give away the bride. The *New York Daily Tribune* of November 7, 1895 observed that Mrs. Vanderbilt had thrown down the gauntlet to her husband's family by publishing, in advance, the list of invited guests. All of this added to the drama of the wedding.

The interior of the church was decorated lavishly with flowers and plants that nearly covered all the woodwork. Garlands of white and pink roses, chrysanthemums, lilies of the valley, orchids, alpine violets, and vines were draped in festoons from the dome of the church to the front of the galleries, and wrapped around the columns; trellises of flowers decorated the walls; arches of flowers graced the chancel; tall stanchions placed at the end of every fifth pew on the center aisle held four-feet-high bouquets of roses and greens. Under the illumination of the gas and electric lamps, the appearance was that of a flower garden.

The posts of the pews on the center aisle that were reserved for Mrs. Vanderbilt's closest friends were hung with tiny cards, fastened with a small piece of white silk ribbon and inscribed with the names of those who were expected to occupy each pew.

Although the ceremony was scheduled for noon, the doors of the church were thrown open at 10:30. Admission was by card only, but this didn't deter some of the socialites from rushing in to get the best seats, some even refusing to take the seats that were assigned to them.

At 11:15, Walter Damrosch conducted a symphony orchestra in Beethoven's *Leonore Overture No. 3*, followed by selections from Wagner's *Die Meistersinger*, until the arrival of Mrs. Vanderbilt just before noon.

As chimes pealed and a crimson carpet was rolled down the center aisle, anticipation rippled through the church and the guests leaned forward in their seats. Alva Vanderbilt, escorted by the head usher and her two sons, did not disappoint them. She was dressed in a sky-blue satin gown, walking length, with a gored skirt trimmed with a three-inch border of Russian sable. The bodice,

embroidered in silver, oval pearls, and pale green leaves, was also trimmed with the same fur, as was her small toque. She carried a muff of blue satin banded with sable and a large bouquet of white roses with long blue and white satin streamers. As mother of the bride, she took her seat in the front pew on the left side of the aisle, along with her two sons.

The Duke of Marlborough, with his best man, came from the vestry next and took their places at the foot of the chancel steps, in front of the pew on the right side of the aisle, which was occupied by the British ambassador.

The groom wore an American-made suit of gray cloth, with a long frock coat. A large white gardenia was pinned to his left lapel. He did not wear gloves. The best man wore a dark frock coat and trousers, with a blue-and-white striped shirt and white collar and cuffs.

The church was still. The moment for the bridal procession had arrived. As one tense minute merged into the next, a slow murmur made its way along the aisles. Where was the bride? The groom was visibly shaken. Although he tried to look unconcerned, he toyed with his mustache, his face almost white. Alva maintained her composure. She had placed a guard outside Consuelo's room and was confident that no one could get near her. What she had not anticipated was a tearful bride, whose swollen eyes had to be sponged for twenty minutes before she could leave for the church.

Finally, at 12:15, the orchestra leader signaled the beginning of the Wedding March from Wagner's *Lohengrin*, the officiating clergy came to the center of the church, the ushers walked down the center aisle to take their seats in the front pews of the side aisles, and the bridal procession began. The eternity of anxiety was over.

The eight bridesmaids marched down the aisle in pairs. Each was dressed identically in walking length white satin gowns with broad sashes of sky-blue ribbon, the same color as that of Alva Vanderbilt's costume. Around their throats was a band of blue velvet and pearls, and on their gowns they wore the turquoise brooches presented to them by the Duke and the diamond butterflies from Consuelo. Their large hats of royal blue velvet had broad brims trimmed with blue satin bows, six large pale blue ostrich tips and a white aigrette, and their bouquets of bride roses and lilies of the valley were tied

with the same blue and white satin ribbons. When they reached the chancel, they formed a double line with four on one side of the aisle and four on the other.

The bride, on her father's arm, looked every inch the duchess she was to become even though she did not wear one piece of jewelry. Her gown of cream-color satin had four tiers of d'Angleterre lace on the skirt, each twelve inches deep, made from designs suggested by her mother. Trails of orange blossoms fell down the right side from a cluster on the top flounce. The corsage with its high-standing collar and long sleeves was embellished with lace and a spray of orange blossoms on the left shoulder. The fifteen-foot court train that fell from her shoulders was embroidered with pearls and silver in a design of rose leaves tied with a true lover's knot. On her hair, which was arranged in a pompadour, a coronet of orange blossoms held a veil of fine Brussels net. She wore embroidered white silk stockings and white satin slippers spangled with silver.

Expanding on the prevailing fashion of the time, Consuelo Vanderbilt carried an enormous bouquet, almost three feet wide, made up of orchids, lilies of the valley, and cattleya ferns that had been cultivated at Blenheim Palace, the duke's ancestral home in Woodstock, England.

As the bride approached the chancel, the groom came forward to meet her and together they passed through the line formed by the bridesmaids to the chancel rail. Her father took his place to the right of the best man.

The service was fully choral. While the party was grouping at the altar the sixty-voice choir, accompanied by the organ, sang:

O! perfect love, all human thought transcending,
  Lowly we kneel in prayers before thy throne,
That theirs may be the love that knows no ending,
  Whom thou forevermore dost join in one.

O! perfect life, be thou their full assurance,
  Of tender charity and steadfast faith,
Of patient hope and quiet, brave endurance,
  With childlike trust that fears no pain, nor death.

Grant them the joy which brightens earthly sorrow,
  Grant them the peace which calms all earthly strife,

And to life's day the glorious unknown morrow
  That dawns upon eternal love and life.

The irony of this could not have escaped those who knew that this was by no means a marriage of love.

Later, after the marriage vows and the prayers, while the bride and groom were kneeling on a white silk cushion embroidered in gold, the choir once again sang, this time the anthem "Deus Miseratur."

When the final words of the anthem had been sung, the bishop gave the benediction and the religious ceremony was completed, but one final act remained, the signing of the marriage register in the formal British fashion. Since this was to take place in the vestry with only the principals, the bride's mother and father, and the British ambassador, Alva Vanderbilt had arranged for a musical interlude in the church. The orchestra played Mendelssohn's music for "A Midsummer Night's Dream," while the bridesmaids distributed roses and pink and white carnations from small baskets to the guests seated in the middle aisle.

Those enjoying this charming pause in the ceremony had no way of knowing that inside the vestry, in addition to signing the register, Consuelo, her father, and the duke also signed a marriage contract that gave the duke and Consuelo $2,500,000 worth of stock in the Beach Creek railway with a guarantee of 4% annual income for life, as well as a separate agreement from her father giving the couple $100,000 a year for life. Alva had accomplished her goal—she had captured a duke for her daughter, and the duke had secured a much-needed source of income to continue his lifestyle at Blenheim Palace. As far as Alva was concerned Willie's responsibilities were now over, and she let it be known that he was not to be present at the wedding breakfast in her home.

The group, minus Willie who left by the side door, re-entered the church. The orchestra played the march from Wagner's *Tannhauser,* and the duke and duchess led the procession down the aisle to the waiting carriage that would take them to the wedding breakfast in Alva's house.

Although only one hundred twenty-five of the guests were invited to the reception and wedding breakfast, the preparations were equally elaborate and perfect in every detail.

In the Vanderbilt house flowers were in abundance everywhere with masses of roses, chrysanthemums, and palms banked to the ceilings. Standing under an immense bell of white flowers, the duke and duchess received their guests in front of a screen of green orchids, while pink orchids and ferns were hung like curtains on the opposite wall of the room.

The two drawing rooms were decorated with American Beauty roses, pink and white roses, and palms. The dining room had a theme of white flowers—orchids, roses, and chrysanthemums. The oval table set for the bridal party had a centerpiece of white orchids, lilies of the valley, and smilax running the full length of it. The candles in the candelabra had white silk shades.

The wedding breakfast was a rather hurried affair. The duke and duchess were to spend a week in seclusion at her father's estate, Oakdale, at Islip, Long Island, and a private railroad car was to meet them at three o'clock at Long Island City to take them there.

The carriage that had driven Consuelo to the church, with the horses, coachmen, and footmen still wearing the white ribbons and flowers on their lapels, was waiting at the curb to take them to the railroad car. The duchess in a dark traveling dress and the duke in his long frock coat came out of the house, followed by ushers throwing rice. As the carriage started on its way, someone threw a pale blue satin shoe at the carriage. It didn't land on the roof, as superstition decreed it must for good luck, but instead hit the coachman's hat. Perhaps this was an omen of things to come, for the duke and duchess were separated in 1906 after only eleven years of marriage.

The British perception of the wedding was quite different from that reported by the American newspapers. In the November 16th issue of the *Illustrated London News,* the Ladies' Page had this to say:

It is certainly proper that the American public has had the sensation of the Duke of Marlborough's wedding, but they have "made terribly much" of it over there. Fancy anything so grotesque—indeed, repulsive—as the bridal party going to the church the day before and having a "rehearsal" of the ceremony so as to be sure that they should make no public mistakes! Fancy the very under clothing and "silk stockings embroidered with silver up the ankles" that the bride was to wear at the wedding being on show! The manners and customs of weddings differ in the States considerably from those of our own etiquette, and not only in such points as those just alluded to, which are mere matters of good taste and feeling. For one thing, their weddings are often celebrated at an impromptu altar in their own drawing rooms, instead of in church, as indeed, the Scotch often arrange their ceremony. For another thing, it is usual for the bride to stand under a canopy or large bell of white flowers, suspended from the ceiling, while she receives congratulations. Again, the groomsman has never gone out of fashion there. He is called an "usher," and in most weddings his duty is simply that of the old-fashioned groomsman—namely, to look after (and if possible flirt with) the bridesmaid to whom he has been individually alloted.

At the Marlborough wedding there was a large breakfast, and an innovation that only millionaires are likely to keep up—the bride presented every guest asked to the breakfast with a souvenir—a handsome jewelled chatelaine for each lady friend, and a tiny watch, small enough to be worn on the lapel of the coat as a "favour" and yet a perfect timekeeper, to each gentleman present. They are much more given to this pretty but expensive custom of providing "favours" for guests in America than we are...but the splendor of these Vanderbilt wedding gifts cannot be regarded otherwise than a true American ostentation of wealth. It inevitably happens that in a country where there is no hereditary aristocracy, wealth becomes the only basis of social superiority, and therefore is flaunted. Here birth, and the manners and culture that it is supposed to imply, can hold their own against money to some extent. So much the grander our estate!

The more staid report in the November 23rd issue of the *Illustrated London News* mentioned the presence of the Governor of New York as well as the staff of the British embassy in Washington. It also noted that Sir Julian Pauncefote, the British ambassador, read telegrams of congratulations from Queen Victoria and the Prince of Wales at the wedding breakfast.

SELINA SMITH and JOHN EUGENE OSBORNE
The Prettiest At-Home Wedding in the History of Princeton, Kentucky

When Selina Smith married John Eugene Osborne on November 2, 1907, it was one of the prettiest "at-home" weddings in the history of Princeton, Kentucky, according to all the reports.

The setting was Adsmore, the Victorian home of the bride's parents, Mr. and Mrs. John Parker Smith, so named because Mr. Smith kept adding more to the house.

Selina Smith was their youngest daughter, described as a typical Kentucky beauty, accomplished and charming, who could move with ease in any society. John Osborne was the ex-Governor of Wyoming, where he owned a ranch; he was a former surgeon for the Union Pacific, member of the National Democratic Committee from his state, and later, named Assistant Secretary of State by President Woodrow Wilson. They had met in Europe while she was on the "grand tour," which so many prosperous families of that time provided for their daughters. What began as an educational experience for Selina, by the end of the trip had become her destiny. She and John Osborne, who was twenty-eight years her senior, were engaged to be married. Her father wasn't overjoyed that she had become engaged to an "old Westerner," but he accepted it.

Although the wedding was at 10:30 in the morning, the curtains were drawn to darken the parlor and the reception hall so that the new electric lighting, of which the Smiths were so proud, could cast a soft glow on the setting. The stair railing was wrapped with ropes of smilax and ivy, accented with honeysuckle and bows of tulle at regular intervals.

The actual ceremony took place in the parlor that had been decorated with a profusion of white chrysanthemums, roses, and ferns. Chairs from the dining room were set up to face the fireplace where the bride and groom would exchange their vows.

When the organ began the traditional wedding march, John Osborne, the groom, entered first, with his best man, the Honorable John W. Gaines, followed by the bride, her sister, Mrs. J. H. Williams of St. Louis, as matron

A formal portrait of Selina Smith, the beautiful and charming bride of John Osborne, seen here in her wedding dress of Brussels lace and Irish crochet over satin and chiffon. (Courtesy Adsmore Museum, Princeton, Kentucky)

of honor, and her little niece, Katherine Garrett, as ring bearer.

Selina, carrying a bouquet of lilies of the valley, wore a gown of imported Brussels lace appliqué and Irish crochet over satin and chiffon, and white satin slippers trimmed with bows of satin petals. Her tulle veil fell from a crown of orange blosoms. The only piece of jewelry she wore was a necklace designed with a diamond harvest-moon pendant, a gift from the groom.

To carry out the color scheme of yellow and white, the matron of honor wore a gown of yellow silk net and velvet with Irish crochet trimmings on the bodice and a large black velvet picture hat. Her flowers were white chrysanthemums.

Katherine Garrett, the little ring bearer, was also dressed in yellow and white. Her white Swiss batiste dress was trimmed with bands of pale yellow shadow-embroidered bows on the yoke and the skirt. Pale yellow silk ribbon was threaded through white beading on the edge of the sleeves.

It was an impressive ceremony performed by the Rev. M.E. Chappell of the Central Presbyterian Church.

Afterward, the bride's parents, her sister Mayme Garrett, and her husband hosted a champagne wedding breakfast. Although the reception was not a lengthy affair, no detail had been left undone. The buffet table in the dining room was made elegant with a cloth of white linen with cut-work embroidery, festooned with small

Selina Smith, like many brides of her era, had a wedding scrapbook. Some were hand-made, others were commercially published like this example. The scrapbooks often had pages of proverbs as well as charming illustrations, with space in which to record all the pertinent information concerning the wedding. (Courtesy Adsmore Museum, Princeton, Kentucky)

bouquets of tulle and lilies of the valley, placed over a yellow cloth that fell to the floor. A handsome silver basket holding white flowers formed the centerpiece, and princess lamps with silver filigree shades covering yellow candles were placed at either end. Refreshments were typical of a Southern wedding—country ham and beaten biscuits. The ice-cream balls served from a cut glass dish were made by Mayme Garrett, a specialty for which she was well known.

The highlight at most Victorian weddings was, of course, the moment when the bride cut the cake. This one was no exception. The beautiful three-layer cake, topped with a spun-sugar basket holding fresh lilies of the valley and roses, had been made in St. Louis and brought to Princeton by train. It was displayed prominently at one end of the buffet table.

As they left the wedding, each guest took a small white box tied with ribbon which held the traditional souvenir of a Victorian wedding, a piece of dark fruitcake. These had been arranged on a beautiful glass cake stand placed on a lace-covered table in the reception hall.

Like many brides of that era, Selina had a wedding book, in which to record all the details of this important occasion. Hers was titled *Cupid's Proverbs—A Wedding Book*, and it contained several pages of proverbs, such as "A word to the wise is sufficient," "Pride goeth before a fall," "Diligence is the mother of good luck." Each was illustrated with cupids. In addition, there were pages of love poems, and still others to record the details of the wedding, including the date, the decorations, and the presents.

Of course, 1907 was not part of the Victorian era. That ended with the death of Queen Victoria in 1901. However, social customs continue and change gradually over time to reflect changing values. The wedding of Selina Smith and John Osborne is a good example of wedding traditions from one era that carried over into the next.

Adsmore, originally built in 1857 and remodeled in 1900 by Selina's father, is now a museum operated by Princeton's George Coon Library Board. Once a year, for several months, it is made to look just as it did on the day that Selina Smith married John Osborne, using all the original decorations.

Ideas to Borrow
from the Past

Ideas to Borrow from the Past

The Victorian wedding of the past was a romantic occasion because every tradition had a purpose and every detail had a meaning of its own. Together, they symbolized the sentimental ideals that the Victorians cherished. These same customs can be borrowed or adapted to make the Victorian wedding of today that much more romantic. Each bride, like those of the past, needs to decide which ideas are the most appealing to her, what traditions she would like to start, and which sentimental memories of her wedding day she would like to cherish in the years to come.

These are some ideas that were appealing to us. You may find others in the chapters of this book.

🌹 Start a family tradition with an exquisite bride's handkerchief that can be put away for future brides in your family to use on their wedding day. If the initial of your maiden name is embroidered on it, that should make it even more valuable from a sentimental point of view. Keep a running record with it of the dates and the names of the brides. It may not matter for the first generation, but it could be very meaningful for the third and fourth generations.

🌹 Select one flower as a theme for the wedding and keep the sentiment of the day always with you by making it your flower for life.

🌹 Think of the bride's bouquet as a love poem that can express your special sentiments and select the flowers that represent your feelings about love and marriage.

🌹 Follow the example of Queen Victoria and use ivy or myrtle in your bouquet, which can then be planted

after the wedding to be used by your children and their children for their wedding bouquets or decorations.

🌹 Create one large bride's bouquet from as many small bouquets as you have attendants; hide a plain ring (it doesn't have to be gold) in one and tie them together with a white satin ribbon. When it comes time to leave the reception, untie the ribbon and give one to each bridesmaid, or throw them if you prefer.

🌹 Have the florist create a marriage bell of flowers to stand under if the ceremony is to be at home. The bell need not be totally covered with flowers. Some can be placed here and there on a frame entwined with ivy or myrtle.

🌹 Identify the occupants of the reserved seats in the church the way Alva Vanderbilt did at Consuelo's wedding. Have the names lettered on elegant little white cards and hang them with narrow white satin ribbons at the ends of the reserved pews.

🌹 Adapt the idea of the wedding favor and give each of the guests as they enter the church a simple white flower tied with a white ribbon to wear at the wedding. If you have selected a flower for life, for example the chrysanthemum, use that for the wedding-favor flower.

🌹 If the marriage ceremony is to be in a church, have the groom escort the bride's mother down the aisle to her seat.

🌹 Or, why not have the bride walk down the aisle alone, preceded by her father and mother walking arm in arm.

🌹 Have little girls, at the end of the service, stand at the ends of a few pews near the front of the church to throw flower petals on the wedding party as they march down the aisle.

🌹 If you prefer having flower girls with baskets to throw petals in the path of the bride as she walks down the aisle, have each one escorted by a little boy dressed as a page, carrying a sheaf of wheat to symbolize fertility.

🌹 Ask a little girl to serve as ring bearer, carrying the ring on a small silver tray.

🌹 If it is a small wedding, especially in an old historic house, have friends and relatives stand in a semicircle in back of, or facing, the bride and groom during the ceremony.

🌹 Arrange for a horse-drawn carriage to drive the bride and groom. Use large bunches of white flowers as favors on the horses and the lapel of the coachman.

🌹 Plan a Victorian wedding breakfast, elegant in all details, served "en buffet," with the bride cutting the first piece of wedding cake as the highlight of the reception. Remember, these breakfasts lasted only one and a half to two hours.

🌹 After the bride cuts the first piece of the wedding cake, instead of serving the rest of the cake to the guests, ask one or two friends to cut the cake into small pieces to be boxed for everyone to take home. Small white or silver boxes lined with a tiny paper doily placed under the cake and tied with a white satin ribbon can be arranged on a large silver tray or an old-fashioned cake stand.

🌹 Have a special bride's cake, in addition to the wedding cake, just large enough for each bridesmaid to have one slice, baked with the traditional fortune pieces inside: a ring, a penny, a thimble, and a button. Make a special ceremony of cutting the cake just for the bridesmaids and ask each to select the piece that she hopes will forecast her fate. The maid of honor should have the first choice, then the bridesmaids in turn, alphabetically by their last name.

🌹 If the wedding is quite informal and the friends who are to witness it are very special, why not ask each to bake one layer of her favorite cake recipe to be added to those made by the others to form a Friendship Cake, like that made for the frontier bride. The cake could be stacked and frosted the day before the wedding. One friend might even decorate it.

🌹 Plan an anniversary of a wedding to recreate the original event, with the bride, the groom, and the attendants in their original wedding clothes. The bride and her attendants should each carry a bouquet and all can form a receiving line to greet guests. If the dresses are somewhat tighter than they were on the original wedding day, letting them out at the seams might be more nostalgic than buying new ones.

🌹 Adapt the idea for the tin anniversary and suggest that each guest bring one fun gift to exaggerate something about the lifestyle of the couple who are celebrating their tenth wedding anniversary.

🌹 Take a sentimental trip to retrace your honeymoon.

🌹 Plan a small marriage ceremony to renew your vows as part of the anniversary celebration. If it is a milestone, like the twenty-fifth, the "groom" might give the "bride" a new ring. If she's sentimental about the old one, the new one can be bought with the intention of adding it to the ring or rings already on her finger.

🌹 Plan to have a bride's cake for each anniversary, baked with a gold or gold-tone ring in it. Make a special ceremony of cutting it for each of the bridesmaids to select their piece.

Customs from the past are not intended to be used rigidly, unless you are planning an authentic Victorian wedding. Instead, they can serve as sources of ideas to create a romantic wedding now that can become part of your nostalgic memories as you celebrate the anniversaries of your wedding. Some may even start family traditions that will be cherished by future generations.

Romantic
Victorian Weddings
+ now +

Victorian Wedding Flowers

Why have a Victorian-style wedding? Because it is fun, it is personal, it expresses individuality, and—it is romantic.

Planning a Victorian wedding gives you the opportunity to pay attention to all the little things that make a wedding truly romantic: learning what the flowers mean sentimentally, presenting gifts to the attendants that have a traditional value, and making your guests more a part of a special day by sharing an unusual experience that was well-planned. Any period wedding (even the 1920s or 1930s) is fun, for it stands out from the assembly-line wedding we have become accustomed to—with the same food, the same music, even the same matchbooks and favors. Contemporary weddings are too often not enjoyable for the bridal party or guests. Sometimes they seem more like a rerun of "Queen for a Day!" Victorian weddings were genteel and refined and were intended to be a celebration that was shared with the guests. Re-creating a Victorian wedding is an opportunity to make your wedding day one that everyone present will always remember with pleasure.

So you want to have a wedding in the Victorian style. How do you make it all happen? There are many ideas that can be borrowed from the past to give wonderfully romantic touches to a contemporary wedding, but everything has to be carefully planned.

For this book we decided to re-create a Victorian wedding at the Hermitage, a Gothic Revival historic house in Ho-Ho-Kus, New Jersey, that is typical of the many historic sites we have included in our book. It is rented out for wedding ceremonies and receptions. We found experts in the field of flowers and food to plan and create the flowers for the bride and attendants and for the reception and to create the food for the wedding breakfast. We then asked our experts to explain the arrangements for the wedding breakfast and to give as many suggestions as they could for receptions at other times of the year and for varying numbers of people. We also researched and found many helpful sources to help you create your own special Victorian wedding.

Probably the most neglected part of modern weddings is the proper and effective use of flowers. Flowers seem to have lost the sentiment formerly attached to them and are generally considered as little more than a decorative accessory to the wedding gown. Receptions these days often have pitifully few or no flowers at all. But flowers are so expressive of sentiment and beauty, and they give a freshness and vitality to a setting. Victorians gave them much thought and treasured them for their symbolic meaning, fragility, and color.

While any wedding would benefit from greater attention being given both to personal flowers and the flowers for the church and reception, in the re-creation of a Victorian wedding flowers become vital.

For the wedding breakfast at the Hermitage, we asked an expert in Victorian floral arrangements, Ellen McClelland Lesser, to make the wedding bouquets and to decorate the room for the reception. In the following material she explains what she did and also makes suggestions for other kinds of weddings. In addition, she offers some pointers concerning what to ask for when dealing with your own florist.

VICTORIAN WEDDING FLOWERS
Ellen McClelland Lesser

When planning the flowers for the early summer wedding at The Hermitage, we decided on 1895 as an appropriate date. In keeping with the style of that period, we chose roses as the floral theme for the ceremony and reception. The theme of the wedding is established by the bride's dress and flowers, so everything is designed with this in mind.

Although the bride's bouquet is always white, the same sort of flowers that are used in her bouquet are used in the attendants' bouquets but in the theme color. This color is then used for the flowers that will decorate the church for the ceremony and the bride's home for the reception.

At The Hermitage the flowers used were primarily pink roses, which were then accented with pink bouvardia. Roses are a particularly appropriate choice for an early summer wedding, for they are at the peak of bloom at that time. Using appropriately seasonal flowers always helps to emphasize the Victorian appearance of the setting.

Changing Attitudes Toward Flowers

Our taste for and attitude toward flowers has changed over the last hundred years. In the late nineteenth century, the ephemeral quality of flowers contributed to their enjoyment. Flowers that lasted only a day were looked on with fondness, for they made that particular day special. Dinner guests were honored with flowers on the table that had been picked just for the occasion of their visit and would not last past that evening. For weddings, the choicest flowers of delicate structure and exquisite fragrance were sought to make that day especially memorable.

Today, we have quite a different attitude toward flowers. We place a high value on longevity. Flowers that wilt, fade in color, drop petals, and cause the vase water to look and smell unpleasant have all but disappeared from florist shops. The longer-lived the flower, the more highly it is prized. This idea was completely foreign to our nineteenth-century forebears. Today, "the flowers were lovely and they lasted such a long time," is the ultimate compliment, for floral arrangements are expected to last a minimum of a week. If an arrangement lasts through two weekends, so much the better. Although wedding flowers need only last one day, delicate, short-lived flowers are seldom offered for sale. Changes in the floral industry over the last hundred years have made it difficult and impractical for florists to handle such perishable items.

In the Victorian period, the local florist had a range of greenhouses and a field of cutting flowers. Here a large variety of flowers and foliage plants were grown. A typical greenhouse might have Parma violets and sweet violets for winter nosegays as well as primroses, pansies, Roman hyacinth, sweet pea, lily of the valley, and jasmine. Ferns, palms, lilies, hydrangeas, gardenias, orange trees, myrtle, and azaleas were grown in pots ready to decorate the church or the bride's home on the wedding day. These are plants that were very popular and readily available to the Victorian bride. Florists are a little reluctant to handle some of these plants now. White flowers are particularly vulnerable to disfiguring brown marks if even slightly bruised. With careful advance planning, however, most of these plants can still be obtained.

Seasonal Availability

Selecting flowers appropriate to the season for your wedding will emphasize the Victorian setting of the wedding as well as the season. The clear demarcation of seasons has been somewhat blurred in the floral industry. Through hybridizing, new, longer-blooming strains have been developed. By controlling the growing conditions in greenhouses it is possible to extend the period of bloom further. Additionally, improved transportation has made it possible for summer flowers grown on the opposite side of the globe to be offered for sale in the middle of winter. One can have lilacs for Christmas as well as in May.

Some flowers are now available the year round. Chrysanthemums, particularly the "football" mums and pompons, were traditionally fall flowers that are now available throughout the year. However, when making a Victorian floral arrangement, the small pompon chrysanthemum would be appropriate only for fall arrangements, and the large "football" and "spider" mums are a most welcome addition to later winter arrangements. Mid-summer flowering lilies are also offered by florists throughout the year. To use lilies appropriately, bypass the modern Asiatic hybrids of yellow and orange with upward facing blossoms and select a species lily such as Rubrum (*Lilium speciosum*), Goldband (*Lilium auratum*), Easter lily (*Lilium longiflorum*), or Madonna lily (*Lilium candidum*). Spring bulbs, such as tulips, freesia, and narcissus are available at least eight months of the year. They are most appropriate for spring arrangements, of course.

Color

Color played an important role in planning the flowers for a Victorian wedding, and one color was often selected as a theme for the floral decorations for the wedding ceremony and the reception. This created a sense of unity. By 1890, a single color would often be carried through all the floral decorations. In 1895, for example, pink flowers in a range of tints and shades were very fashionable for spring weddings. You will see examples of a primarily pink floral scheme in the photographs of The Hermitage. In 1900, yellow became the fashionable floral color.

A century of hybridization has expanded the range of color in many flowers. For the most part, the change is subtle. Clearer, brighter white flowers have replaced the varieties that tended to be slightly off-white. Many flowers in the Victorian period were actually buff or pale lavender rather than true white. The magenta that is found in so many flowers in the wild was abhorred. Lavender and mauve, however, were perfectly acceptable in the middle of the nineteenth century. But, as hybridizers began to develop clear red, rose, and blue blossoms late in the century, they were much preferred and therefore sought after.

In planning the flowers for a Victorian wedding, stay with pinks, rose, soft yellows, light blue, lavender, and mauve. The beautiful coral, peach, and salmon flowers that are available today are just too modern as are many startlingly bright colors available now. The bright orange

Detail taken from the photograph of the parlor at The Hermitage in Ho-Ho-Kus, New Jersey, decorated for a wedding breakfast. This illustration shows the floral decoration of the chandelier above the buffet table. (Photograph by G F Studio/Rob Kern)

Window decoration in The Hermitage parlor done by Ellen McClelland Lesser. (Photograph by G F Studio / Rob Kern)

• 88 •

Because the wedding breakfast in The Hermitage parlor was created in June, the hearth was also beautifully decorated. (Photograph by G F Studio / Rob Kern)

'Tropicana' rose, for example, is an intensely hot orange color that is beautiful in fall arrangements but was beyond anyone's wildest dreams in the nineteenth century. Keep in mind that russet, olive, and maroon were perfectly acceptable colors in 1880.

The Table

In the Victorian period flower arrangements were not limited just to the center of the table, but often reached to the corners and encompassed the entire length of the table. In the center of the table illustrated is an 1895 version of a two-tiered arrangement. Although the two-tiered style of floral arrangements had been in vogue for some time, this particular type was originally designed by R. Felton in England and named for the actress Ellen Terry, who was well known for her appearances in plays by George Bernard Shaw. The original design called for a ball of moss enclosed in poultry mesh to be placed on top of a metal rod attached at the bottom to the center of a shallow tin dish. A similar stand can be made today with floral foam wrapped in poultry mesh and placed on top of a wood, plastic, or metal rod.

The arrangement shown is composed of fern fronds, springeri, rose foliage, and pink roses. Ivy, jasmine, and honeysuckle could also be used. Maidenhair fern is the most authentic fern, but if this is not available, then leatherleaf fern is also suitable. Bits of rose branch are trained down (or up) the center post. Additional long pieces attached to the arrangement trail toward the corners of the table. If the arrangement sits under a chandelier, a pretty effect is achieved by twining a piece of vine in the fixture so that it trails down to the center arrangement.

"Specimen" glasses or flutes about eight inches high are set at the corners of the table, and they are filled with a few sprigs of greenery and some roses.

Window Decoration

Swags of foliage are draped across the top and down the sides of the windows in the dining room. The swags are composed of Western sword fern, huckleberry branches, and long branches of rambling rose, and are accented in the corners with pink roses. All the plants are inserted into floral-foam blocks attached to the corners of the window frames.

A ball of greens and roses is suspended from the center of the swag. Originally, this would have been made of poultry mesh surrounding dampened sphagnum moss. Our floral ball is made with a styrofoam ball covered with leatherleaf fern, huckleberry branches, and rose foliage. The roses and rose foliage are held in plastic tubes called "water piks" that have been inserted into the styrofoam. Vines trail from the window swag so that it appears as though the ball is held in place by the vines rather than by wire.

Fireplace Decoration

Inasmuch as this has been planned as an early summer wedding, the fireplaces would not be used. It was customary in the summer to cover the empty fireplace with a decorative fireboard. For our wedding the hearth is made handsome with an arrangement of pink flowers framed with a background of huckleberry branches, leatherleaf fern, and Western sword fern. The tall flowers at the back of the design are a double-pink form of bouvardia. The clusters of tiny starlike flowers provide a pleasant contrast to the shape of the roses. Although this is essentially a "rose" wedding, the use of a few other flowers, where appropriate, creates a nice counterpoint to the roses.

Potted plants such as a large Boston fern or pink hydrangea would be equally attractive on the hearth. A large fireplace might also be flanked with potted palms.

Cake

The wedding cake is decorated with gardenias and lilies of the valley around the base. Both real or artificial flowers work well as decoration.

The decorative flowers should not be pressed into the decorative icing on the cake, for when the cake is ready to be cut, it is best if the flowers can be lifted off without spoiling the appearance of the cake. Florists have special containers that sit on the top of the cake and/or in the spaces between the layers.

The wedding cake made by Susan Lang Simon is decorated with gardenias and lilies of the valley. (Photograph by G F Studio/Rob Kern)

White roses are used to make this bouquet for an 1895 bride. (Photograph by G F Studio/Rob Kern)

In this lovely bouquet—called a posey—for an 1870 bride gardenias are combined with sweet peas, stephanotis, and lilies of the valley. (Photograph by G F Studio/Rob Kern)

PERSONAL FLOWERS

Types of Bouquets

Spray—in the nineteenth century this was a large bouquet with an irregular outline. It was a popular style in the 1890s and early 1900s. *Posey*—a circular, small hand bouquet, now called a nosegay. *Nosegay*—a hand bouquet constructed with concentric circles of flowers. *Colonial Bouquet*—a large version of the nosegay. This is not a term used in the nineteenth-century floral books. *Cascade*—today, this is a pear-shaped bouquet, wide at the top and narrow at the bottom. In 1890, it described a bouquet that was like a waterfall of flowers that could extend almost to the hem of the skirt.

Bride—1895

For the most part, bridal bouquets in 1895 were exclusively white and they often contained only one type of flower—white roses, lilies of the valley, orchids—or a

combination of two types of flowers—orchids and lilies of the valley, stephanotis and lilies of the valley. Some bride's bouquets were enormous, resembling a fountain of flowers that reached from the waist to the hem of the skirt—absolutely glorious looking but very awkward to carry. A bouquet, more modest in size in keeping with our late twentieth-century sensibilities, which was also recommended to the 1895 bride, was used for the June wedding at The Hermitage. Called a chatelaine, it is oval in outline and has a rounded profile. We made our bouquet using large-headed roses of the variety 'Bridal White,' which is a modern hybrid tea rose of a soft ivory white. At least two dozen roses must be used to achieve a full effect. The rose foliage is the only greenery needed. At the center of the bouquet are four or five partly open roses in a cluster. Surrounding these are single roses in tighter bud placed at irregular intervals until a generally oval shape is achieved. Attached to the bunch of roses are ribbon streamers with a rosebud knotted randomly along the streamers. For the bride's bouquet, the ribbon must be of fine quality and of a pale ivory color to match the roses. The important finishing touch for the bouquet is to wrap the holder with the same ribbon just as it would have been done in 1895.

Attendant—1895 (Adult)

The attendants' bouquets are similar in design to the bride's bouquet—only a little less grand. If there is a color theme for the wedding, it should be brought out in the attendants' bouquets. For the wedding at The Hermitage, we used pink sweetheart roses. Again, there is a central cluster with individual roses placed toward the edges. And again, the only greenery is the rose foliage. The streamers are made from pale green ribbon with a rosebud knotted here and there along the length. It is better to use light green ribbon rather than pink or white. For a bouquet of pale yellow roses, however, white ribbon is the first choice, followed by pale yellow or blue. The attendants' bouquet holders should be wrapped with either pink or pale green ribbon.

Attendant—1895 (Child)

Little girls were included in weddings in the nineteenth century just as they are today. Their flowers should be

Bridal Pink roses were used to create this bouquet for an 1895 bridesmaid. Note the rosebuds knotted in the pale green ribbon streamers. (Photograph by G F Studio/Rob Kern)

This charming bouquet for an 1870 bridesmaid contains a gardenia, roses, lavender sweet peas, stephanotis, and lilies of the valley. (Photograph by G F Studio / Rob Kern)

appropriately small and easy to carry. We suggest a pomander, which is a small ball of flowers with a bow at the bottom and a bow at the top, with the top ribbon extending into a loop that serves as a handle.

Men

A simple white rose boutonniere would be appropriate for the groom. Today, all the men in the wedding party are given boutonnieres just as it would have been done in the nineteenth century.

Headpieces

The Victorian bride usually wore a circlet of orange blossoms on her head as a symbol of chastity. Today, stephanotis is substituted when orange blossoms are not available. Bouvardia with its clusters of tiny trumpet-shaped flowers can also be used effectively.

Evergreens

When used to festoon the galleries of the church in summer these could be mountain laurel, arborvitae, rhododendron or magnolia foliage. In winter, the festoons might be made from mountain laurel, holly, boxwood, princess pine, or any other locally available Christmas green such as pine, spruce, juniper, or cedar. Arborvitae and mountain laurel are usually available all year round.

Greenery for decorating the inside of the house would often be of a more refined nature. Typical materials are springeri, ivy, smilax, jasmine, and honeysuckle.

Myrtle

The myrtle that Queen Victoria carried on her wedding day was of the genus *Myrtus*, one of a group of tender shrubs with fragrant leaves and fragrant white flowers. It is not *Vinca minor*, the running-myrtle or periwinkle that is commonly used as a groundcover plant. The correct sort of myrtle can be purchased as a potted plant from herb growers and garden centers, if the local florist has none available.

A BOUQUET OF HINTS FOR WORKING WITH THE FLORIST

Book a florist as early as possible. At the time of booking it is important for you to provide basic information about the size of the wedding and the scale of the decorations envisioned. In this way the florist can reserve an appropriate amount of time to prepare the bouquets and decorations. Wait until the bride's wedding gown and the attendants' gowns have been selected so that swatches of the fabrics are available before settling on any of the details of the bouquets or decorations. The flowers should, of course, complement the bride's gown and those of her attendants.

Very few illustrations of bouquets or other floral decorations are to be found in bridal magazines. The best illustrations can be seen in books at the florist shop. Often shops have an album of photographs of weddings that they have done as well as the large volumes produced by the wire services. Make an appointment with the florist to spend some time just looking at such books.

Try not to schedule a visit to the flower shop during the week before a major holiday. At that time, shops are so busy that no one can give you the attention that you deserve.

Although a Valentine's Day wedding may sound very romantic, flower shops are so busy and the demand for flowers so great that you will not get the best service or value. Mother's Day and Easter should also be avoided for the same reason if at all possible.

If you are using potted plants to decorate the church or reception, beware! The plants come in black plastic nursery pots or inexpensive green plastic pots, both of which are inappropriate and unsightly. Often the pots are wrapped in shiny foil of various colors, which is also not appropriate. Ask to have the plants put into terra-cotta pots or set in gold- or silver-colored baskets.

Victorian bouquets were trimmed with a fine satin ribbon. Ribbon today is usually made from synthetic materials and often has a cut/fused edge. For a Victorian-style bouquet, ribbon should have a woven edge. This is a better-quality ribbon that looks more finished and makes a softer bow. If the florist cannot supply a paper frill to back the bouquet, a heavy-weight paper doily could be used instead.

Although baby's breath both fresh or dried is very popular today, it was seldom used in nineteenth-century table arrangements or bouquets.

Since flowers come from all over the world, it is not possible for a florist to guarantee that some of the more unusual flowers will be available on a particular day. Florists make their best effort to fulfill your requests. To avoid disappointment it is best to offer alternatives to your first choices. Be sure to tell the florist if there is a flower that you do not like as well as those that you prefer—and any other likes and dislikes that would affect the floral decorations. Rustic baskets, which are so popular in "country look" arrangements, are not suitable for table arrangements in the Victorian style.

If there are special or sentimental items that you would like to include in the floral decorations, bring them to the florist to look at and take measurements, but do not ask the florist to take the responsibility of keeping them until the wedding. Containers of particular value can be fitted with an inexpensive plastic liner, the arrangement made in the liner, and then delivered in the liner to the ceremony or reception and set in the special container there.

Although it is more costly to have a florist set up the flowers rather than just deliver them to the reception, it is well worth the extra expense. While setting up, the florist can add the few extra flowers and make the slight adjustments that make the floral arrangements look just perfect in the space allotted to them.

ELLEN McCLELLAND LESSER of Stuyvesant, New York, is a horticultural historian. She studied horticulture and landscape architecture at the University of Massachusetts and commercial floral design at the New York Botanical Garden. Re-creating nineteenth-century floral arrangements combines her interest in nineteenth-century plant materials and aesthetics with a life-long love of arranging cut flowers. She has served as a consultant to museums and historical associations. Her floral designs are featured annually at Olana, the home of the great nineteenth-century artist Frederic Edwin Church in Hudson, New York. She may be contacted by writing to Post Office Box 147, Stuyvesant, New York, 12173.

Food for the Reception

With respect to the food for the wedding reception there are, of course, many factors that will determine the appropriate menu: time of day, number of guests, season, and the amount of money available. When planning a Victorian-style wedding much depends on the amount of time you wish to spend on making the food traditional. To some couples, the food is an important part of the reception; to others, just providing a variety of foods that guests will enjoy is sufficient. It would, however, break the mood of the period wedding if some attention was not paid to the types of food and their proper presentation. It is not a big budget that will make the food a wonderful part of the reception, but rather it is attention to detail and good planning. For our wedding breakfast at The Hermitage we asked a food expert, Catherine Titus Felix, to plan a buffet menu for us that would be correct for an 1895 wedding, would not be too expensive, and would look attractive.

Catherine prepared all the food herself, so we know it can be done and that it also tastes good. We asked her to discuss her preparations for our wedding breakfast and to give some suggestions for other kinds of receptions.

VICTORIAN-INSPIRED FOOD FOR THE RECEPTION
Catherine Titus Felix

Today's bride may not have the family cook at her disposal as she would have had in the nineteenth century, but a Victorian-style wedding party can still be offered.

Victorian wedding receptions were usually held in the bride's home. The scale of the reception was, of course, dependent on the size of the family home and amount of help available. If the family was wealthy and had a large house and staff, then a quite lavish presentation could be offered. If the home was more modest, then the food was prepared by the family and servants and extra help was hired for the day if needed. Cakes and some other items such as ice cream were often bought in shops when available. But it was only in the latter part of the nineteenth century that professional caterers were employed. The reception, or wedding breakfast as it was called throughout most of the century, was a lovely, genteel celebration of a marriage.

Service

The buffet service preferred by Victorians for a wedding breakfast has a lot to recommend it over a served, sit-down meal. From a catering standpoint it is preferable to prepare a variety of dishes that hold up well for self-service than to try to serve a hundred people the same meal at the same time. Many of the foods that were typically served at a buffet can be prepared well in advance and frozen, making it possible for a bride, her family, and friends to do some or all of the cooking. You won't need as many people to serve and clean up after a buffet as you would for a sit-down meal.

Our Victorian ancestors consumed copious amounts of butter, salt, and cream without concern, but it would be very rare today to entertain a large group of people without finding a few guests on restricted diets. With a buffet you can accommodate these guests by including dishes that are universally acceptable such as fresh fruit, salads, vegetables, and breads. Then your guests can help themselves to what they are able to eat without feeling embarrassed or deprived.

One departure from authenticity you will probably

want to take is in the seating of your guests at tables. The Victorians did not always provide for this but no one enjoys juggling drinks, plates, forks, and napkins while standing. If you must invite more people than you can accommodate at tables, restrict your menu to tidy finger foods or those that require only a fork, and try to have enough chairs for everyone.

• 96 •

Working with a Caterer

You will need to decide on your budget before you meet with a caterer. Be sure to be realistic about the cost of food. When catered, most foods cost four to five times as much as the sum of their raw ingredients. Consider the expense of rented equipment; will you be able to accommodate your guests inside or will you be renting a tent? Chairs, tables, cutlery, and so forth can all be rented, but obviously they add to the cost. In most areas, party planning services are available. Such a service will help you with all the details, and make all the arrangements.

You are especially lucky if you have an acquaintance who can recommend a caterer. Otherwise you will find listings in the yellow pages for party planners, caterers, and florists. A few phone calls may be required before you find someone who is interested in a historic project. Have a clear idea of what you want and then meet with the caterer. Some organizations are more flexible than others, so if you don't find someone who "speaks your language" right away, don't give up. Ask for references, ideally of people who have had similar events.

A "small" caterer may be more flexible than a bigger company. However, many such caterers are not licensed by the board of health, which means they haven't proven their knowledge of safe food handling, and haven't had their kitchens inspected. They may not have the equipment to keep large quantities of food cold and hot, both absolutely necessary to insure the safety of the food, so be sure to check. It is worthwhile asking if the caterer is fully insured; food poisoning is no joke.

Having any historic party catered is a lot like getting historically sensitive work done on your house; some people know what you're talking about and are interested, others are not. And just like having work done on your house, the best way to find a true craftsman is to network with friends.

Selecting a Menu

The Victorian bride was restricted by the season when making her menu selections. It's worthwhile keeping that in mind if you are aiming for authenticity. Although improvements in transportation after the Civil War extended the availability of many items, fresh peas, tomatoes, and strawberries, for example, would not have been available in the winter months.

Few people have access to a consulting food historian when planning a wedding breakfast, but you can consult actual nineteenth-century cookbooks and their reprints. Cookbooks proliferated in the late 1800s, and many of these books offered sample menus to guide the novice hostess through the tricky maze of Victorian etiquette. Menus for festive meals usually followed the structure of an eight-course dinner even if they were served buffet style. The actual progression of the courses varied, but the menus often featured oysters, soup, fish, entrée, meat, game, salad, and dessert courses.

Menus

The three menus that follow are based on advice and recipes drawn from three volumes in my collection of nineteenth- and early twentieth-century cookbooks. I have assembled menus that I hope will appeal to people today. The recipes chosen appear in the books credited. I have tried to capture the "flavor" of each era without being slavishly historical and have included brief descriptions of the dishes where needed.

BEFORE THE CIVIL WAR
A Spring Dinner of the 1860s from Mrs. Haskell

In her 1860 cookbook Mrs. E. F. Haskell sets out to go "…minutely into many things…" including how to entertain guests stylishly. The menu that follows is based on her outline for a "genteel dinner," which at that time required six courses and took for granted that there was a servant at hand. Her advice was for a sit-down dinner, but the menu also lends itself to a catered buffet. This is not the kind of food that would have been served for a wedding breakfast, but it would make a nice substantial wedding dinner with the addition of wedding cakes. The menu could be used for a large rehearsal dinner as well.

Menu

French Vegetable Soup

A puréed-vegetable soup of brown stock, potatoes, parsnips, onions, and carrots seasoned with salt, pepper, mustard, and catsup—I would substitute tomato paste for the catsup.

Boiled Salmon with Cucumbers in Vinegar

Poached is a better description of the cooking process. Mrs. Haskell served this warm, but it would be delicious cold. The cucumbers should be thinly sliced and seasoned with salt, pepper, and vinegar and served as a relish or garnish.

Roast Turkey

Mrs. Haskell recommended an oyster sauce for the turkey, but her recipe doesn't sound too appealing. Most people probably would prefer having gravy available.

Roast Lamb with Mint Sauce
Mashed Potatoes New Peas Cranberry Jelly Celery

Lettuce Salad

This was dressed with hard-boiled egg yolks that had been combined with mustard, salt, pepper, butter, and vinegar. You could substitute a good vinaigrette.

Vanilla Blancmange with Strawberries and Cream

Fruit and Nuts

Wedding Cake or Cakes

Coffee

You will need a caterer to look after the roasts and accompaniments, but if you wanted to do some of the preparation beforehand, the soup could be made in advance and frozen. The day before the wedding you could poach the salmon and make the blancmange.

THE GILDED ERA
A Winter Wedding Breakfast of the 1880s from the White House Cookbook

The opulence of the Gilded Era was as evident on the dining table as it was in the decorative arts. With the addition of entrée and game courses, the formal dinner had expanded to include eight to twelve courses, each offering a variety of dishes. While it was never actually fashionable to be stout, a few extra pounds was a conspicuous sign of wealth, and this was certainly the era of the conspicuous.

It was the heyday for New York's famous restaurant, Delmonico's, and for gourmands like Diamond Jim Brady and Lillian Russell (America's sweetheart weighed two hundred pounds). Stylish menus were written in French, although the food represented on them was not necessarily French. Dinners were expected to last at least two hours and what genteel ordeals they must have been. It is difficult to imagine how Victorian ladies managed as many as twelve courses while wearing corsets.

The publishers' preface to the *White House Cookbook*, first published in 1887, stressed that each recipe had been "...tried and tested..." This may explain why the book was so successful and also widely plagiarized. The menu that follows is lighter than an authentic one for the period would have been, but each item can be found in that book and would have been available during the winter months. This menu is particularly well suited for do-ahead preparation at home. The soup, turkey, and squash can all be kept frozen for a week or two. Smoked salmon can be purchased, ready-sliced, at a good delicatessen, fish market, or supermarket. The potatoes, celery, and orange slices can be made one day ahead. Buy a good-quality ice cream, and have the cake baked for you.

Menu

Hot Consommé

Smoked Salmon

This was broiled and then thinly sliced. I would skip the broiling and serve it thinly sliced on toast points. Offer lemon wedges and capers as a garnish.

*Turkey Scallop

The recipe in its entirety is offered below. This could be very tasty if made with layers of poached turkey, bread crumbs, and a good velouté sauce.

Potatoes à la Delmonico

Melon-ball-size rounds of potatoes steamed in butter.

Baked Winter Squash (mashed)   Stewed Celery

Orange Slices

Ice Creams   Nuts   Cakes

Coffee

*TURKEY SCALLOP

The recipe, exactly as it appeared in the *White House Cookbook*, follows. The lack of specifics: how much turkey, milk, bread crumbs, and so forth, illustrates the kind of challenges that a Victorian cook faced. I have included the recipe more for inspiration than duplication.

"Pick the meat from the bones of a cold turkey and chop it fine. Put a layer of bread crumbs on the bottom of a buttered dish, moisten them with a little milk, then put in a layer of turkey with some of the filling, and cut small pieces of butter over the top; sprinkle with pepper and salt; then another layer of bread crumbs, and so on until the dish is nearly full; add a little hot water to the gravy left from the turkey and pour over it; then take two eggs, two tablespoonfuls of milk, one of melted butter, a little salt and cracker crumbs as much as will make it thick enough to spread on with a knife; put bits of butter over it, and cover with a plate. Bake three-quarters of an hour. Ten minutes before serving, remove the plate and let it brown."

THE TURN OF THE CENTURY
An Elegant Wedding Collation for Summer
From Mrs. Rorer, *Ladies' Home Journal*, 1902

Sarah Tyson Rorer was the principal of the Philadelphia Cooking School and the author of nine cookery books when her *New Cook Book* was written in 1902. In that volume she pleads for simple dinners, denouncing the feasts of the previous decade as "…feedings, extravagant, coarse and vulgar." She also suggests that it is possible to entertain guests for dinner without a servant but concedes, "This is, of course, a difficult task…" There are very few menus in Mrs. Rorer's book, but she does mention that salads can be served as the main course for "…evening affairs, or wedding collations…" I have taken her cue and offer the following menu that would work well for a large number of people and again offers the possibility of home preparation. The sandwiches, lobster, bean, and tomato salads could be purchased at a delicatessen or made by a few willing friends the day before. The chicken timbale can be made and frozen. It is served cool, so it just needs to be defrosted and garnished. The sherbet and cake can be handled as mentioned above.

Menu

Lobster or Crab Salad

*Chicken Timbale

String Bean Salad

Tomato and Cucumber Salad

Sandwiches

Raspberry Sherbet

Olives   Nuts   Candies

Punch

Wedding Cake

Coffee

*CHICKEN TIMBALE
(serves 8 to 12)

This is adapted from a 1902 recipe by Sarah Tyson Rorer. Mrs. Rorer confined her seasonings to just salt and pepper for this molded-chicken dish. I have jazzed that up a bit, but otherwise this is a fairly authentic interpretation of her recipe. She suggested serving it warm with a mushroom sauce, but I think for a wedding buffet it would be easier to offer it cold and accompany it with a mayonnaise. The timbale freezes well so it can be made up to one month in advance; defrost it slowly in the refrigerator.

1 cup hot milk
1 cup fresh white-bread crumbs
2 lbs skinless, boneless chicken breasts
2 eggs
1½ tsp salt
¼ tsp pepper
2 small shallots, chopped fine
1 Tbs chopped fresh parsley
¼ tsp dried thyme
⅛ tsp grated nutmeg
3 Tbs cognac

1. Pre-heat oven to 350 degrees. Thoroughly butter a decorative 2-quart mold.
2. In a small bowl, pour hot milk over crumbs and let stand 10 minutes or until milk is absorbed.
3. Chop chicken in a food processor until coarsely ground. Add crumbs and then remaining ingredients. Process until well combined.
4. Spread chicken mixture evenly into the prepared mold. Cover mold tightly with aluminum foil. Set mold in a large roasting pan. Add boiling water to pan until water level reaches halfway up the sides of the mold. Bake in pre-heated oven 1½ hours or until internal temperature reaches 165 degrees when tested with a meat thermometer. The time required to reach 165 degrees will vary according to the shape of the mold, so it is important to check, for *underdone chicken is not safe to eat.*
5. When done, remove mold from oven and set on a rack to cool. Top it with a plate that will fit within the mold and sit right on top of the chicken. Place a 2 lb weight on the plate (a couple of cans of beans work well here) and allow the mold to cool until easy to handle. Put the mold in the refrigerator after it has cooled, and chill until cold. Remove weight.
6. To unmold: Set the mold in a basin of hot water, being careful not to splash water inside. When the gelatin and fat around the edges become liquid, lift mold from basin, top with a serving plate, and invert. Remove mold. The timbale may be frozen at this point, after it has been well wrapped.
7. Garnish to suit your color scheme. For instance, use tomatoes or radishes with a red pepper- or tomato paste-flavored mayonnaise for a pink and white color scheme. Watercress, hard-boiled egg quarters, and yellow chrysanthemum blossoms with herbed mayonnaise make an attractive green and yellow presentation.

Victorian-Style Menus
I have developed the following menus to reflect Victorian style without worrying about authenticity. With these menus you can focus on the decorative aspect of the food,

A Yellow, Green, and White
Wedding Luncheon

Smoked Mackerel Pâté
(the recipe for smoked salmon pâté can be used with any smoked fish)

Deviled Eggs

Rolls with Butter

*Chicken Timbale

*Asparagus Vinaigrette

*Apricot Mousse
(this is a pale golden yellow)

Wedding Cake

Punch   White Wine or Champagne   Demitasse

uniting its color scheme with the bridesmaids' gowns and flowers, a practice that did not come into vogue until sometime after 1900.

*ASPARAGUS VINAIGRETTE
(serves 6)

2 lbs asparagus
1 red bell pepper
1 clove garlic
¼ tsp salt
1 tsp Dijon mustard
3 Tbs red-wine vinegar
⅓ cup olive oil

1. Peel the stalk ends of the asparagus, trimming away any really woody parts. Bring 2 to 3 inches of water to a boil in a saucepan large enough to hold the asparagus lying down. Put the asparagus in the boiling water and cook 5 to 7 minutes, or until softened through but not completely limp. Drain and refresh.
2. Meanwhile, slice red pepper into ⅜" rings. Cook in boiling salted water until softened, drain, and run under cold water to refresh.
3. Allow asparagus and pepper to cool completely while preparing vinaigrette dressing.
4. Crush garlic in salt (a mortar and pestle is handy for this). Mix in the mustard, and then the vinegar. Whisk in the olive oil. Whisk again just before using.
5. Arrange asparagus in a serving dish, wrapping into little bunches of 3 or 4 spears with red pepper rings.
6. Coat evenly with the vinaigrette dressing and refrigerate for 30 minutes or more.
7. Bring to room temperature before serving.

Variation: Omit red pepper, and top with a finely chopped hard-boiled egg just before serving.

*APRICOT MOUSSE
(serves 6)

Molded, gelatin-set desserts were very popular with the Victorians, and were usually included in lavish menus. Preparing this sort of dish is a cinch today thanks to reliable gelatin, refrigerators, and food processors.

¾ cup dried apricots
¼ cup white wine
¼ cup water
⅓ cup sugar
½ tsp almond extract
⅛ tsp salt
2 Tbs lemon juice
1½ envelopes plain gelatin
3 Tbs water
4 eggs separated
½ cup heavy cream
additional whipped cream
   for decoration (optional)
a few mint leaves for garnish

1. Prepare a decorative 6-cup mold by lightly oiling it.
2. Combine apricots, wine, and ¼ cup water in a small non-reactive saucepan and simmer gently, tightly covered, until apricots are very tender, about 25 to 30 minutes. Add more water if things start to look dry in the pan. Purée the apricots with sugar in a food processor until very smooth, transfer to the bowl of a heavy-duty mixer, add almond extract, salt, and lemon juice.
3. Sprinkle gelatin over 3 Tbs water in a small saucepan or microwave-safe dish. Set aside to sponge until gelatin has absorbed water—about 10 minutes.
4. Add egg yolks to the apricot mixture and whip at highest speed until very light, thick, and fluffy—about 5 minutes. Melt gelatin over low heat or for 1 minute at 60% power in a microwave. Pour into the mousse base and mix well. Mixture should be very thick; if it isn't, set the bowl into a larger bowl of ice and water and stir until almost set.
5. Whip egg whites and heavy cream. Fold into the mousse base, combining well. Pour into the prepared mold and refrigerate 2 hours or overnight. Turn out onto a serving dish and decorate with whipped cream and garnish with a few mint leaves.

Menu

A Pink and White Wedding Tea

Wedding meals were never called teas. The terms used were *breakfast, collation, reception, luncheon,* or *dinner,* but never *tea*. Still, the kind of food most often served for a tea party would be lovely for a wedding, and the bride and caterer can be as creative as they like. You might enjoy adding to this menu sandwiches made with paper-thin slices of Virginia ham, thus making it a "high tea."

Plain Scones with
Clotted Cream, Crème Fraîche, or Whipped Butter and
Strawberry Jam

Cucumber and Watercress Sandwiches

Ribbon Sandwiches

Meringues with Strawberries and Cream

Wedding Cake

Tea   Dry Sherry   Champagne   Coffee

Menu

An Indian Summer Buffet

The harvest is in, and the beautiful colors of autumn offer a wealth of decorative possibilities. These are the inspiration for the following menu.

Consommé with Puff-Pastry Fleurons

Crab Cakes

Chicken Provençale

Saffron Rice   Green Beans   Mashed Butternut Squash

Olives   Nuts   Bonbons

Chocolate Charlotte Russe

Bride's Cake   Groom's Cake

Blush Wine   Punch   Demitasse

The Foods that Made the Feast

Throughout the nineteenth century oysters and lobster were almost inevitable menu items for special events. Our pristine waters yielded a plentiful, cheap, and seemingly endless supply of these delicacies, and they were not the luxury foods they are today. Raw oysters were sometimes served as an hors d'oeuvre, but more often as an extra course. Lobster, in a dizzying variety of guises, appeared as the fish course. Many of the recipes for lobster I have found in the old cookbooks are wildly rich, and just too much for today. Salmon, shrimp, sole, turbot, cod, and flounder were also popular. Chicken and turkey were very expensive, so they were often the highlights of lavish menus. Veal, sweetbreads, and kidneys were regular offerings for the "entrée," which was the course served before the roasts.

Gelatin-set molds were fascinating to our ancestors. Commercially prepared powdered gelatin was available in the 1840s, but apparently not widely marketed. The need for good refrigeration to set jellied foods put them in the luxury class. By the 1870s middle-class people had efficient iceboxes, and in the 1890s gelatin powder was mass-marketed. Molded items were then not only luxurious, they were modern—who could resist?

Frozen ice creams and ices were also popular party foods that benefited from technical advancements. Although ice cream has been popular since the earliest days of our republic, it wasn't until the invention of a portable ice-cream maker in 1848 that it became accessible to everyone. This machine was such a success that by 1850 ice-cream was deemed a party necessity by *Godey's Lady's Book*. Including it in your menu will be an authentic touch.

An assortment of simple sandwiches, nuts, olives, and candies dispersed along the buffet table were regular features of Victorian menus that can easily be duplicated today.

Beverages

For beverages the nineteenth-century wedding hostess usually offered a light red wine, champagne, punch, and demitasse. Mixed drinks did not exist, and straight hard liquor was never served. The punch recipes encountered in nineteenth-century cookbooks tend to have quite a high alcoholic content. Today, Americans are drinking less alcohol than ever, so a nice touch here would be to offer a pretty, nonalcoholic punch.

I prefer to serve a first-rate domestic white or blush wine to an inferior champagne no matter how traditional it is. So unless your budget is up to a really good champagne, I always recommend a good still wine.

Regardless of the beverages served, the serving pieces can maintain a Victorian ambience. A beautiful punch bowl, ladle, and cups, coffee served in dainty demitasse cups, with an antique sugar bowl and creamer, and the prettiest wine glasses you can find will all help create a nineteenth-century atmosphere.

• 102 •

Presentation and Garnish

With all of your menu selections, be sure to garnish lavishly. As with most decorative items, the Victorian view on garnish was that more was better. No daintily perched, tiny portions of color coordinated vegetable purées for them! Try to offer platters piled high with food and festooned with parsley or watercress. In her *New Cook Book*, Mrs. Rorer suggests a garnish of fringed celery (celery that is cut into two-inch lengths with the ends cut closely six to eight times. When set in cold water these ends will then curl). Carrots, nasturtiums, violets, rose petals and leaves, chopped radish, sprigs of mint, hard-boiled eggs, crawfish, and shrimp are also cited as possible garnishes. Nothing was brought to the table without its own complementary garnish.

The old cookbooks don't often mention what to use for garnishing specific dishes, but do say it is important to do so tastefully. I suggest you choose a garnish to correspond with your color scheme, and a garnish should always reflect the contents of the dish it is complementing. For example, a seafood salad could be effectively served in split, hollow lobster shells that are nestled on a bed of watercress or curly parsley, and the border of the platter could be surrounded with crayfish or shrimp.

Doilies were used with abandon in the late nineteenth century, and are very pretty in paper or cloth. If you have access to some beautiful, antique serving pieces by all means use them. Nothing is more effective for giving a table a Victorian look than lots of sparkling cut glass and gleaming silver. Don't worry about everything matching. A full set of matched china was certainly dear to the heart of every Victorian hostess, but surviving period photographs testify to the frequent use of mismatched pieces.

Linens

Fine table linens are also important for creating a Victorian atmosphere. If authenticity is of interest to you, you may be disappointed. Throughout the nineteenth century fine linen damask was considered the only appropriate cloth for a formal table. Those magnificent lace creations (see the color plate on page 62) were only used for luncheon and tea.

In the pre–Civil War era the damask cloth was spread over a colored cloth, which was exposed when the damask was removed before dessert. Later in the century, the damask was placed over a thick pad of baize or cotton flannel, and only the crumbs were removed before dessert. The napkins used were large, heavy linen damask.

These general rules applied to buffets as well, although in the late nineteenth century the table was often skirted to the floor for a buffet.

Another fashion was for tulle, silk, or organdy to be swagged around the edge of the table, and the swags were fastened to the damask with ribbons or flowers.

By the turn of the century, lace centerpieces and doilies were occasionally placed on top of the damask for really festive buffets.

If you're more interested in a Victorian look than a historic re-enactment, I suggest using a really good lace tablecloth, with a colored cloth beneath it to match your color scheme. If you have access to napkins edged with lace, by all means use them. Otherwise get the thickest and biggest napkins you can. If your wedding breakfast is to take place before dark, you can appease your sense of authenticity by the fact that lace would have been used in the daytime.

Another little Victorian touch is using the pretty candle shades that were popular from about 1890 to 1920. These are increasingly available at decorating shops, but the shades can easily be made of a fabric to suit you. You will still need the metal "followers" that sit on the candles and support the shades.

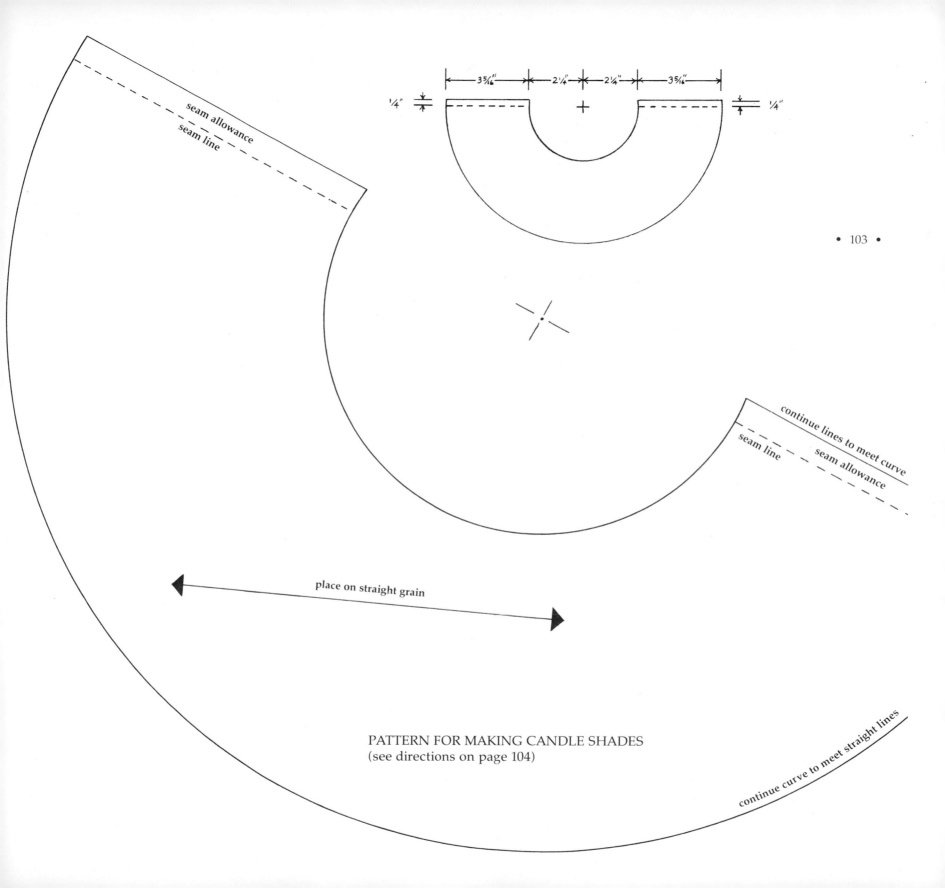

seam allowance
seam line

3⁵⁄₁₆″ 2¼″ 2¼″ 3⁵⁄₁₆″

¼″   ¼″

• 103 •

continue lines to meet curve
seam line   seam allowance

place on straight grain

PATTERN FOR MAKING CANDLE SHADES
(see directions on page 104)

continue curve to meet straight lines

To Make Candle Shades

This pattern was made from an antique shade that I took apart.

You will, of course, need the metal followers to sit on the candles and support the shades.

Place a sheet of tracing paper on the pattern on page 103 and trace it with an indelible marker.

Iron extra-heavy-weight fusible interfacing onto the wrong side of the fabric you have chosen.

Place the pattern on the fabric, aligning the grain lines. Pin it in place, and cut the fabric out carefully. Cut out as many shades as you wish in the same manner.

The seams may be glued or stitched. The top and bottom edges can be finished with ribbon, seam binding, or light-weight trim. The bottom edge should be able to support a light-weight fringe if your interfacing is firm enough.

Carrying a Victorian flavor through to the food served at your wedding reception will complete the ambience you've begun with your gown, flowers, and decoration. Modern dishes presented in a Victorian style can be offered, but there is a straightforwardness to many of the authentic foods that is very appealing. With careful

Menu

Bill of Fare 1890s June
Wedding Breakfast "En Buffet"

Sandwiches

Chicken Croquettes

Jellied Ham

Shrimp Salad in Tomatoes

Olives   Nuts   Bonbons

Strawberries and Cream   Strawberry Ice

*Bride's Cake and Groom's Cake

Champagne   Blush Wine   *Punch   Demitasse

menu selection, garnish, and presentation your wedding breakfast can reflect a nineteenth-century setting and please your twentieth-century guests.

The wedding breakfast in our photographs is set in a June of the mid 1890s. The menu is not an exact re-creation of a historic wedding breakfast, but each item has a historic reference. We had decided on a pink, green, and white color scheme, so I chose food to co-ordinate. I wanted to compose a menu that would be historically accurate, but also appealing and do-able for today.

I eliminated the oysters, although they would have been authentic, because I just can't recommend them for everyone. Many people are allergic to shellfish, and others just don't find oysters appetizing. If you live in an area where *safe, fresh* oysters are available and affordable, and you know that your guests will enjoy them, by all means add oysters to the menu given.

I also eliminated the soup course because I don't enjoy hot soup on a warm day. If you wish to include a soup in your buffet, serve it in cups so your guests can sip it one-handed.

The sandwiches that I prepared for the wedding at the Hermitage were herbed-cheese and a cream cheese with strawberries, but cucumber, watercress, or salmon pâté would all have been authentic and good. For a late summer buffet you could include sandwiches of thin tomato slices with salt, pepper, and butter. The Victorians were very fond of white bread, and rarely offered sandwiches using brown or whole-wheat bread. I included some whole-wheat sandwiches for visual variety. When preparing sandwiches for this type of meal, the bread should be thinly sliced and the crusts removed.

I decided to offer chicken croquettes because I like them, and they are pretty and authentic. There are so many possible ways to serve chicken authentically; poached and sliced with an herbed mayonnaise, à-la-king in puff-pastry shells, a boneless, rolled ballontine (boned meat, fish or fowl that is rolled into a bundle-like shape and served sliced). The suggestions in the menus above are only a few ideas.

I selected a jellied-ham dish for the gelatin mold because of its appearance. As mentioned above, the Victorians loved molded, gelatin-set dishes. Including such an item in your menu will give the buffet a nice period look. There are so many delicious jellied foods, but many of them have been lost in the sea of marshmallow-studded "fruit salads" that washed across our country in this century. A tomato aspic, cucumber, chicken or salmon mold would all be good candidates for this slot in your menu.

If you would like a cool, jellied dessert, nothing could be more appropriate than a Charlotte. These luscious confections of gelatin-set, flavored custards or fruit purées with whipped cream were created by the great chef Carème. Carème served as chef to George IV at the Brighton Pavilion. The desserts were named in honor of Princess Charlotte, George's ill-fated heir, who would have reigned instead of Victoria if she had not died in childbirth.

The ice or sherbet that I included can be tricky to serve. Consider having it scooped ahead into individual dishes or, not authentic but nice, into pretty cookie or chocolate shells. Frozen, these keep nicely overnight. They then can be placed on service plates and brought out after your guests have had their fill of the main dishes. Another option would be to freeze the ices in decorative molds. Victorian menus often feature ice-cream bombes, mousses, and other molded, frozen desserts. These can be individual molds, turned out onto plates and garnished with edible leaves or flowers, or large ones brought to the table on a plate and cut like a cake.

I used a fine linen-damask cloth, placed over a pink skirt reaching to the floor. The ruffled candle shades are made of pink taffeta, resting on metal supporters that have a decorative pattern punched in them. You may have luck finding these at flea markets.

*Pineapple Punch
(6 servings)

From Fanny Farmer's *Catering for Special Occasions*, published 1911.

2 cups water
1¼ cups sugar
1 can (I assume large) crushed pineapple
Juice of 4 lemons
1 quart ice water

1. Boil 2 cups water and the sugar together until all the sugar crystals have dissolved.
2. Add pineapple and lemon juice. Allow to cool, then strain. Add ice water.
3. Pour over a piece of ice in a punch bowl and garnish with thin slices of lemon.

*Bride's Cake
(Two 8-inch square layers)
(serves 12)

The 1906 edition of the *Boston Cooking School Cookbook* carried this recipe. I have adapted the Bride's Cake for modern cooking methods. The cook was directed to bake this recipe in "deep, narrow pans," so presumably it was meant to be cut up and served in squares.

2½ cups flour
1 tsp baking powder
¼ tsp salt
¼ tsp cream of tartar
½ cup butter
1½ cups sugar
½ cup milk
½ tsp almond extract
6 egg whites

1. Pre-heat oven to 350 degrees. Prepare two 8-inch square cake pans by buttering them. Line each bottom with a square of waxed paper, butter again, then sprinkle evenly with flour.
2. Sift together the dry ingredients onto a sheet of waxed paper. Set aside.
3. In the large bowl of an electric mixer, beat butter until light and creamy, beat in sugar gradually. Continue to beat until fluffy, about 4 to 5 minutes.
4. Combine milk and almond extract. Gently beat ⅓ of the flour mixture into the creamed butter, then ½ the milk. Continue until last ⅓ of flour has been added.
5. Beat egg whites until stiff but not dry. Fold into batter.
6. Pour batter into prepared pans and bake 25 to 30 minutes or until delicately browned, and the cake layers pull from the edges of the pans, and the cakes are firm in the center.
7. Cool completely and frost with any white butter frosting. Cut into 2-inch squares and serve on a silver tray or in a silver basket.

Dressing for the Wedding

You may be fortunate enough to own an heirloom Victorian wedding gown, or you may be thinking about buying a vintage gown. There are, however, some real drawbacks to wearing an antique gown. We have asked an expert in the field, Janet Low Rigby, to give us her thoughts on the subject. Here is a discussion of some points to take into consideration if you are planning to wear a vintage wedding gown.

THAT PERFECT DRESS
Janet Low Rigby

The very mention of a "Victorian" wedding creates images of a beautiful bride clothed in a long white gown made of yards of silk and lace. The desire to re-create a wedding from another era is often accompanied with the lovely thought that great-grandmother's 1882 wedding dress would be just perfect for the occasion. If you find yourself with such thoughts, there are several points to be considered before you make such an important decision. A correct choice could mean the difference between the most romantic day of your life—or the most embarrassing.

Old dresses are very much like old people. After they are a hundred years old, they shouldn't expect to go to too many parties. After a certain age, the structure of all textiles weakens. The chemical and mechanical processes involved in producing silk, cotton, and wool fabrics accelerates this natural aging process. Even fabric that has been well cared for probably has hidden problems that could surface unexpectedly.

In the late nineteenth century, silk fabric was weighted with chemicals that gave it body and a better drape. Unfortunately, the weighting process undermines the integrity of the fabric. The added weight puts a strain on the silk fibers and can eventually break them. Mercerized cotton was treated with a caustic potash or soda. Wool was also treated with chemicals for dyeing and finishing.

Over a period of time, the chemicals in the fabric react to humidity in the air and acids in their storage containers, and they change to chemical components that erode the fabric. Even if your heirloom dress appears to be perfect now, chances are that rips and tears may appear as soon as the first fitting or, perhaps, while you are saying "I do."

Most dresses are not in perfect condition. They are marked with the good times of past parties or with the results of improper storage. Most fancy dresses were never meant to be wet-cleaned so stains were never removed. Stains from perspiration, spilled drinks, and street dirt darken and harden with age. To try to clean a dress at home only invites disaster. The chemicals in the fabric often react with the cleaning agent. An aunt's favorite chemical concoction that usually removes every stain might enlarge the spot or even destroy the fabric. Most professional dry cleaners and conservators will not accept the liability of cleaning such a garment. Those who will try will be expensive and their results are not guaranteed.

Insect damage and the overall yellowing from the acids in a wooden or cardboard storage container usually damage the fabric so much that it will never be able to measure up to our twentieth-century ideas of cleanliness.

Then there are places that rent period wedding gowns for special occasions, and they have been tested for strength, and cleaned and repaired. Unfortunately, most of those pieces have become lifeless from too much wear.

The fit of an old dress is also an important factor. Although the health movement in the Victorian period was actively encouraging women to eat properly, to exercise regularly, and to loosen their tight corsets, the truth is that many women had been wearing their corsets from an early age. Their rib cages never developed fully because of the constant pressure. Back widths were smaller than ours today so to fit into a period dress is a physically difficult task. The corsets also compressed their waists to an unimaginably tiny size. Saundra Ros Altman of *Past Patterns* says it is important to wear a corset that matches the style and period of your dress. Imagine, if you would, a 1990s business dress over 1870s underpinnings (bustle and all). Reversing that idea, an 1840s dress would not look right over an 1900s corset.

You would probably have to wear a corset in order to wear a period dress successfully. If you decide to do this, tighten the corset at the waist only, for a completely tightened corset could bruise your ribs. Wear the corset for a full day before you make your final decision. Some women have no problems, but some women will pass out. Decide if you are comfortable enough in a corset to enjoy your special day. Remember you will have to stand for the ceremony and in the receiving line and also dance at the reception.

There are, however, some excellent alternatives to wearing an antique wedding dress. We are experiencing a great Victorian revival. Many commercially available dresses incorporate stylistic elements of the late nineteenth century. Bustles, leg-of-mutton sleeves, and yards of fabric worked into drapery and trains are all styles as romantic as a wedding day itself.

Another suggestion is to make the dress of your dreams. Whether you do it yourself or hire a seamstress, be sure to give yourself enough time to get it just right. Many patterns and fabrics are available by mail, but deliveries can take up to thirty days. Allow an additional four to eight weeks for sewing and another two or three weeks for alterations and unforeseen events. All in all, a custom-made wedding dress is very rewarding because you can decide about exactly what you want. First, decide whether or not you can do the sewing yourself.

You may be an excellent seamstress, but you may not have ample time in which to create your own wedding dress in addition to all the other things that have to be accomplished. If this is the case, find a good seamstress. She can create a pattern from your heirloom dress without taking it apart. (If you live near a living-history museum that has costumed guides, ask the head of the costume department to recommend someone. A list of free-lance seamstresses is often available.) Another option is to use one of the many fine commercial patterns made from original dresses. Most companies that carry historic designs have at least one wedding-dress pattern, although other fancy-dress patterns can be adapted.

Finding the right fabric can be great fun as well as frustrating. Decide if you simply must have silk or whether another fabric will do as well. So many of the new synthetics are very nice, not as expensive, and are easier to care for than silk. If you do decide that silk is what you must have, you are in good company because it is the royal family of fabric. You must plan on paying more for the luxury of having silk. Less expensive silks are often found in the fabric districts of large cities. Be daring and take a day to explore. Many mail-order companies carry silks at reasonable prices. *Sew News* and other magazines geared to advanced seamstresses carry advertisements for a number of fabric companies. Again, be sure to give yourself more time than you think you'll actually need.

Don't plan on wearing an old veil or headdress, for it can be ruined with perspiration and styling mousse. Have a copy of it made along with your dress. As for white gloves, no proper lady would dream of receiving her guests without them.

Spruce up a new dress with elements of the past. Consider using items that will not be subjected to wear and tear. Antique jewelry adds a beautiful touch to a great dress. Have a jeweler check for loose stones or loose clasps.

So, then, what do you do with great-grandmother's wedding dress in the trunk? Cherish it. Remember, it cannot be replaced. Keeping an old dress safely is not that difficult. If, however, you don't want the responsibility, contact your state or local historical society. Most institutions welcome the gift of documented articles from the local area. Don't try to spruce up the dress, but, instead, let them look at it just as it is. Write down as much information as you can about the dress (who wore it, when was it worn, where did they live, etc.). Keep a copy for yourself and enclose one copy with the dress (don't use any pins, just place the information on top of the dress) and send another copy with a covering letter to the curator of the society. Don't be discouraged if the gown is refused, for many institutions already have more wedding outfits than they can take care of. A refusal by an institution certainly does not mean that the dress has no value. Why not keep it yourself? It's not that hard. Just remember the following points.

Heat, moisture, acid, and insects are the greatest threats to an old dress. Consider purchasing an acid-free container and acid-free packing paper to provide the ideal storage environment. (While you're at it why not buy two sets—the second set being for your new dress.) The firm called Cherish (P.O. Box 941, New York, New York 10024-0941, telephone: 212-724-1748) sells the correct storage boxes and packing paper. Pack the dress by padding the folds with tightly rolled wads of paper. Lay sheets of paper between the layers so that buttons, hooks and eyes, etc., will not catch on the fabric. Prevent insect damage by pouring para (dichlorobenzene) moth crystals into a piece of clean, preferably white, cotton fabric and tie it into a bundle. Place the bundle on the top layer of tissue, never directly on the fabric, and close the lid. Put the storage box in the back of your closet. Don't put it in an attic, where temperatures are extreme, or in a basement, where accidental flooding will ruin it if the humidity doesn't. A good rule of thumb for storing clothes is: If the environment is comfortable for you, it is comfortable for your clothes. Ideally, the temperature should stay between 65–75 degrees wth a relative humidity of 50–60%. Check the dress every year (on your anniversary) especially for insects. Replace the crystals every year.

Dry cleaners offer a "wedding dress preservation" service. Check to be sure that all the materials are *Acid-free* and *free of dyes*. Avoid any colored paper (which will run if it gets wet) or vinyl bags (which will trap moisture and encourage mold growth).

Imagine being able to show and tell your daughter and granddaughter about your great-grandmother's dress and your wedding dress that was inspired by it. They may appreciate them so much that you will find you have started a family tradition that they will follow. What a nice thought!

Janet Low Rigby has been involved in various aspects of historic clothing for over a decade. She has worked with many living-history museums and private individuals in the areas of collections management and reproduction of period clothing.

If you do possess a family heirloom or want to wear a vintage garment, there are ways to make it wearable, comfortable, and attractive for today. However, a project of this sort does require personal consultation, and it is not inexpensive. The results, with a really good restorationist or dressmaker, can be quite rewarding. Here are some excellent sources in the field.

ANTIQUE GOWNS

Carolyn Niezgoda
Heirloom Wedding Couturiere
8743 21st Avenue
Brooklyn, New York 11214
(718) 946-6652

Carolyn Niezgoda's work is devoted exclusively to the art of restoring and refashioning antique wedding gowns. Niezgoda says that she has "a deep appreciation of old and fine craftsmanship. I see each piece as a work of art to be developed and handled with respect, love, and integrity."

She can work with a variety of beginnings: a family heirloom, a family wedding gown that a bride may want to wear for sentimental reasons but that needs style and decoration, or the "find" from the vintage clothing store that just doesn't make it when you get it home. With her long experience in fitting and tailoring, her personal collection of antique lace and fabric, and her extensive creative abilities, Niezgoda can fashion a beautiful new garment from the old.

Before she accepts an assignment, the gown is carefully examined to determine its potential and whether it meets her criteria. Can it be washed? Can it be resized to fit properly? Are the laces repairable? Can the weakened areas be rewoven? Does the gown have the tensile strength for another wearing? If the garment passes the initial tests, then the consulting can begin.

Just some of the things Niezgoda does to create a unique gown are: Resize for proper fit, redesign sleeves and neckline, set a new waistline, create additional length, add such details as lace insertions, flounces, etc. Niezgoda can also design and create a headpiece to go with the gown, and sometimes even accessories such as glovelets, garters, etc. are created from finds.

The most important part of the process is the collaboration with the bride-to-be so that the final result will prove to be the dress of her dreams. Niezgoda has a file full of thank yous and wedding portraits from grateful brides. In fact, she is often invited to the wedding, and it was at one such wedding that we found her. Carolyn Niezgoda often consults through the mail and by phone with clients living outside New York City.

Helene Von Rosentiel, Inc.
382 11th Street
Brooklyn, New York 11215
(718) 788-7909

• 109 •

One of the boutiques in Michelle's New Hampshire shop features two one-of-a-kind wedding gowns newly created from antique laces, together with old hat boxes, hand-decorated shoes, and a bouquet of preserved roses. (Photograph of Michelle's shop © 1990 by Leslie O'Shaughnessy Studios)

This custom restoration service can restore antique gowns for wearing again. First, the prospective gown must be seen and its age, wearability, and general condition and appearance are taken into account. Then the project is discussed with the client and detailed suggestions are made. The gown, if not too fragile, can be made to fit, made more flattering, even changed somewhat in style. It is often possible to change the gown and then readapt back to its original style. At least one, and possibly two, more fittings are necessary. Custom headpieces are made from restorations or newly created. Von Rosentiel does museum-quality restorations, and this is custom work of a meticulous nature. She feels that it is best to begin work approximately four months before the gown will be worn.

Michelle's
58 Depot Road
Box 314
Hollis, New Hampshire 03049
(603) 465-3286
and (summer)
3 Salem Street
Nantucket, Massachusetts 02554
(508) 228-4409

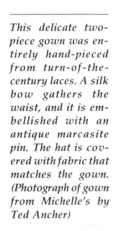

This delicate two-piece gown was entirely hand-pieced from turn-of-the-century laces. A silk bow gathers the waist, and it is embellished with an antique marcasite pin. The hat is covered with fabric that matches the gown. (Photograph of gown from Michelle's by Ted Ancher)

Michelle's is a full-service bridal boutique specializing in magnificent, one-of-a-kind bridal gowns hand-made from antique laces and linens. Fourteen years ago, out of her frustration with antique gowns that were just too fragile to be restored, Michelle Callahan designed a blouse made from old laces, which was the beginning of the concept for her wedding dresses, that are all based on the idea of a blouse and a skirt. Each two-piece wedding gown is created by hand from antique laces, linens, embroidered tablecloths, and other old textiles.

Michelle's shop, which is located in a renovated barn in back of her house, is full of bridal accessories such as fancy headpieces, hand-decorated shoes and beribboned hats, as well as her one-of-a-kind wedding gowns, all displayed in boutiques that were formerly stalls for the horses.

Unlike most of Michelle's gowns, this one, which is created from a magnificent banquet cloth, is in one piece, which is fitted and with a high neck. The fabric is linen with elaborate inserts of shaded filet crochet. (Photograph of gown from Michelle's © 1990 by Leslie O'Shaughnessy Studios)

The two-piece linen gown illustrated in these two photographs is made from fabric that dates back to 1860. It is heavily detailed with Venetian needle lace, filet crochet, and extraordinary hand embroidery. On the front of the gown there is a scene of a gentleman proposing to his lady. (Photographs of gown from Michelle's by Steve La Badesa)

MAKING YOUR OWN WEDDING GOWN

There are many advantages to making your own wedding dress. Probably the most important is that by doing so you can design it to be just the way you want it. You can trim it exactly as you want—as little or as much and in just the right places. It is also much easier to have the gowns for the attendants to be similar in style and period if they are all handmade. There are also patterns available for the men in the bridal party and even for the guests. Even if you buy fairly expensive fabric, the total expenditure will still be less than what you might pay for a readymade gown. Making your own gowns, particularly with the help of the attendants, can also be a lot of fun and it gives the wedding a real individuality.

The drawback, of course, is that you must be a good seamstress. However, it is possible to have the wedding outfits handmade even if you're not a sewing expert. It is usually not that hard to find a good seamstress. The seamstress at your local dry cleaner, tailor shop, or department store is sometimes far more talented than she (or he) gets the chance to show. If you start the project well in advance, it could prove a welcome part-time job for a local seamstress.

Many large and small cities have an area that specializes in wholesale fabric and trimmings for bridal outfits that will also sell retail. For instance, in New York City, within the famous Garment District there is the Trim District, which has many shops in the area around West 38th Street between Fifth and Sixth Avenues. Among these shops are Cinderella, Max's Bridal, and Paul's Veil and Bridal on West 38th Street, or SposaBella on West 40th Street. You can buy ready-made hats and veils or veiling and trimming with which to make your own. Check the yellow pages for your area for listings of such shops and also look for theatrical costuming shops where you can often buy unusual fabrics and trimmings.

Wearing a Victorian gown frees you from worrying about what is in fashion this year, what the latest colors are, etc. When making your own dress, you can more easily choose the most flattering style from the period that you like for your own age and type. For instance, many brides I have spoken to chose a ball gown because they wanted the off-the-shoulder look (particularly

A two-piece linen gown with filet-crochet inserts and pale pastel embroidered flowers that could be worn by a bride or a bridesmaid. A panama hat with large cabbage roses completes the look. (Photograph of gown from Michelle's by Ted Ancher)

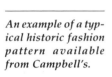

An example of a typical historic fashion pattern available from Campbell's.

Campbell's has a forty-eight-page catalog of historically authentic and period-inspired fashion patterns, including an Edwardian wedding dress by Folkwear and an 1885 wedding dress by Past Patterns. There are many varied and interesting items in this catalog in addition to the patterns: Battenberg lace kits, sewing accessories, corset kits, books, stationery, unusual buttons. The catalog is $4.00 and a free brochure is also available.

Past Patterns
Saundra Ros Altman
P.O. Box 7587
Grand Rapids, Michigan 49502-1014
(616) 245-9456

Saundra Altman makes patterns from original garments or original patterns. She researches the clothing by

flattering for the ample bosom), the small waist, and the big, hip-hiding skirt of the ante-bellum era. It is, of course, one of the most romantic looks possible. If you want a simple summer wedding breakfast, possibly at a bed and breakfast inn or at home, you could choose a simple Edwardian-style dress of lawn or any light-weight sheer cotton and give it most of its period look with flowers, a headpiece, and other accessories. You can have a high neck if you like, short or long sleeves, simple or elaborate detailing, all by picking a pattern from the era you like most and in the most flattering style.

Campbell's
R.D. 1, Box 1444
Herndon, Pennsylvania 17830
(717) 425-2045

Drawing of a tunic dress of the 1880s available from Past Patterns.

studying museum collections (and many of her patterns are duplicates of gowns or patterns in museums or historical collections), tailoring manuals, and seamstresses' workbooks. Saundra not only knows about the fit of women's clothing from the 1830s through 1914 but she also actually wears the clothing from the underwear out to test the fit of the garment during various activities.

There are many beautiful bridal dress patterns available, both from the Victorian and Edwardian periods. The patterns have suggestions for pleasing variations on the pattern as well as which fabrics are appropriate. The corsets are also available in pattern or kit form. Many Victorian and Edwardian dresses will not look as they should without the proper shaping of the undergarment such as chemises, petticoats, and drawers. Just reading a Past Pattern catalog gives the reader a short course in the history of clothing of the period. The catalog is also nicely illustrated.

Send $3.00 for the Victorian and Edwardian Catalog to the above address. Saundra Altman is constantly adding to her collection, however, so don't hesitate to call her if you have specific needs.

Patterns of History
State Historical Society of Wisconsin
816 State Street
Madison, Wisconsin 53706

Eight women's costumes, dating from 1835 through 1896, are included in this series. They were drafted from garments in the collection of the State Historical Society of Wisconsin, and they were adjusted to fit modern women without corsets. They represent the most common cut of each period and may be dressed up or down according to the material and trim used. Suggestions come in each packet for fabric and color choices, accessory and hair styles, and some information about the women who originally wore the garments. A separate bustle pattern is offered for use with the 1876 dress. A gentleman's three-piece sack suit is also available. Although none of these patterns is for a wedding dress, two or three of them would work nicely as a wedding dress if made in the right fabric. But they are all wonderful ideas for the wedding party and guests. Send a stamped, self-addressed

• 115 •

Here is another period pattern—a wedding dress from 1893—to be found at Past Patterns.

envelope for a free brochure with illustrations of all the costumes and an order form.

New Columbia
P.O. Box 524
Charleston, Illinois 61920
(217) 348-5927

For special-period Victorian wedding re-creations, such as a Civil War wedding, New Columbia's catalog of military uniforms will be useful. The precise patterns are from the period 1800–1875. Send $3.75 for an illustrated catalog.

This delightful collection of objects in Victorian style is typical of the wearable art created by Connie Simmerlein at Vintage White.

Amazon Drygoods
Janet Burgess, President
2218 East 11th Street
Davenport, Iowa 52803-3760
(319) 322-6800

The slogan for this unique company is "Purveyors of needed items for the 19th Century impression." Just some of the items available to help create that impression (and selected for their appropriateness to weddings) are listed below.

Patterns: Patterns from the Past. Catalog — $4.00. Includes patterns for some very elaborate and beautiful gowns that would be wonderful as wedding gowns, including an 1859 Flounced Ballgown, an 1862 Rose Petal Ballgown, an 1864 Young Lady's Dress, a two-piece 1880s Bustle Ballgown, and many more. There are patterns for a Gentleman's Sack Suit, and some charming patterns for children's outfits that would be wonderful for weddings either as part of the wedding party or as a guest. There are also patterns for corsets (even in large sizes), corset covers, crinoline covers, and plain and elliptical petticoats. Patterns for accessories include lace mitts, a fan with braid design, and a parasol cover.

Readymade items: Garters, corsets, stockings, shoe tassels, hoops, collars, fans, crocheted bag, and ostrich plumes are just some of the pieces available.

Shoes: Amazon Drygoods has high-button shoes in 500 colors! Bone is so popular that they keep them in stock in all sizes. The waiting time for custom orders has been cut down to three to six weeks, but do leave yourself plenty of time before the wedding. Shoe styles include scalloped high-button shoes, an Empire pump, and spats.

Books: The amazing variety of books offered in the general catalog ($2.00, and it includes the shoes and readymade items) is so varied that it is actually a library of books on Victorian clothing, furniture, sewing, children's books, etc. Two recent additions are books on the language of flowers and the language of fans. For those who are really serious about making their wedding clothing authentic, books can be found on tailoring, lace, and all related topics.

Note: While it was not originally created as a wedding dress, my favorite item in the varied Amazon line is a pattern for a dress called "The Barbecue Party." The barbecue-party dress was worn by Vivien Leigh as Scarlett O'Hara in the film *Gone with the Wind*. It was designed by Walter Plunkett, who spent months traveling to historical societies and private collections in the South, where he examined and sketched original costume pieces from the Civil War period. The green color of the printed sprigs on the white fabric ground was chosen to enhance Vivien Leigh's eyes. This is a wonderful and very popular dress, and it is in the Costume and Textile Department of the Los Angeles County Museum of Art. The pattern replicates the dress and is authorized by the museum. What a wonderful dress for the maid of honor or for the bridesmaids!

RENTING

An alternative to the restored antique, the handmade, or readymade gown is to rent one for the occasion. This is not, however, recommended without reservation. The

From the Laura Ashley Bridal Collection a multitiered wedding gown in cotton sateen.

This simple brides-maid's dress from the Laura Ashley Bridal Collection is made of white cotton with a full tea-length skirt.

CUSTOM MADE

Suzanne Klodowski
289 Harristown Road
Glen Rock, New Jersey 07452
(201) 447-1468 (after 6 p.m.)

Custom sewing for the entire wedding party. Copies of historic dresses, as well as new creations in the Victorian spirit.

Marilyn Hamill
2233 Buchanan, S.W.
Grand Rapids, Michigan 49507
(616) 245-9460

Makes authentically styled wedding gowns.

Vintage White
Connie Simmerlein
P.O. Box 433
Lakeland, Florida 33802-0433
(813) 682-1834

gowns may look a bit worn and may have been incorrectly altered. However, if you can find a good source, it is worth a try. The only source that has come to our attention that we can recommend is an unusual firm on Long Island that is a veritable treasure trove of all manner of Victorian items and clothing.

Antiques at Trader's Cove
Nan Guzzetta
Port Jefferson, New York 11777
(516) 331-2261

From this amazing emporium you can rent anything from a bridal gown to costumes for the entire bridal party and guests. Nan has a huge warehouse full of vintage clothing with everything a period wedding would require. But it doesn't stop there. She also has props of all kinds: furniture, linens, even a horse and buggy. It is necessary to consult with her well in advance. She has shipped items for weddings all around the country.

Connie Simmerlein creates wearable art in vintage styles. She can create a new piece of jewelry using a family heirloom as the basis for the design. Lacking an heirloom, Connie will create a new piece that looks like an heirloom. She can also create shoes, hats, headpieces, and other accessories that will give a period accent to the wedding costume. She also has a large collection of vintage clothing and trimmings. Her unusual Wedding Heirloom Collection begins with a custom-designed invitation, using the bride's colors or theme, and incorporates keepsakes, family photos, family heirlooms, slippers, purse, and jewelry, and all are designed so as to be handed down for generations.

BUYING READYMADE

Laura Ashley Bridal Collection
Available at Laura Ashley stores around the country.

When thinking about buying a wedding gown, and if you

favor simplicity, then take a look at the Laura Ashley Bridal Collection. While the gowns are not replicas of Victorian gowns, they are similar to the simpler bridal dresses of the nineteenth century. With the addition of a more Victorian- or Edwardian-style headpiece (which you must make or have made) and flowers done in period style, the dresses make a good basis for that romantic vintage look. They are simply designed in cotton, lawn, cotton brocade, and cotton sateen, but the details of bows, puffed sleeves, fabric flowers, dropped waists, and cascading bustles give a period stylishness to the simplest of them. One gown, in cotton lawn, is quite reminiscent of the Southern Belle type with off-the-shoulder sleeves and large bows, and another version has delicate lace detailing and satin-edged roses. Attention is also paid to the bridesmaids, including a white dress that is very much like the white ones worn by nineteenth-century bridesmaids. One of the best things about the Laura Ashley Bridal Collection is what is missing from it—the kind of glitzy nightclub look of so many far more expensive gowns in readymade lines today. Laura Ashley shops that carry the Bridal Collection have a Bridal Consultant available to help select the right combination of bridal and attendants' gowns. Laura Ashley also has a Bridal Registry in the Laura Ashley and Home Shops.

There are some other readymade lines that have some Victorian-inspired gowns such as Priscilla of Boston and Gunne Sax. Jessica McClintock and Mary McFadden's Children have some lovely costumes for children in the bridal party to wear. These lines are all regularly featured in bridal magazines and in bridal shops.

THE BRIDE'S TROUSSEAU

Westminster Lace (a group of twenty-seven lace-specialty stores each in a romantic Victorian setting)
Headquarters: 1326 Fifth Avenue
        Suite 646
        Seattle, Washington 98101
        800-262-LACE

Part of the romance of the Victorian wedding is the selection of the bride's trousseau, which in Victorian

This ring-bearer's pillow, traditionally carried by a young boy, is made of silk with an overlay of handmade lace, and decorated with beads and sequins. (Westminster Lace)

• 119 •

Modern brides who want to follow the Victorian tradition of carrying an elegant handkerchief that can be handed down to other generations can choose between an elaborately embroidered one or one with a deep edging of handmade lace. This linen handkerchief, hand embroidered in hearts and flowers, is made in Madeira. (A limited edition from the private collection of Westminster Lace)

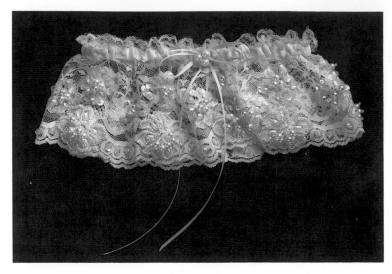

Because catching the bride's garter is a challenge for un-married men at a wedding, an elegant garter could become an heirloom for his future family. This one is made of French Alençon lace trimmed with beads and sequins.

times meant not only her wedding dress and delicate undergarments, but at least a ten-years' supply of house-hold linens as well. The sentimental bride selected some items that could become family traditions from one generation to the next, along with the practical linens needed for housekeeping.

The Westminster Lace stores offer an abundance of lace-touched treasures for the bride's trousseau from beautifully detailed bridal accessories to one-of-a-kind linens for the home. Many of the laces have been created from antique patterns exclusively for Westminster Lace.

GLOVES

LaCrasia Creations, Inc.
Jay G. Ruckel
6 East 32nd Street, 6th floor
New York, New York 10016
(212) 447-1043

Jay Ruckel has a huge collection of antique gloves. Most of the nineteenth-century gloves he owns are crocheted. Queen Victoria loved to crochet, and so it was a popular Victorian pastime. Ruckel points out that it is very difficult to tell newly crocheted gloves from antique examples because the new ones have such an old-fashioned, delicate look. Fashion plates from the Victorian era tended to go into great detail about the

dresses, but rarely mention the gloves. Of course, we know from antique-costume collections and some fashion plates that brides often wore kid gloves at formal weddings. However, they are extremely expensive today. LaCrasia has some charming white crocheted gloves that are decorated with lace and pearls. Actually, LaCrasia has any type of glove you can think of, including kid gloves in all lengths and colors, because they are one of the premier glove makers in the fashion industry. Ruckel suggests that brides- and bridesmaids-to-be consider taking a bit of lace they may be using to trim a dress and appliqué it onto a plain cloth glove to create an old-fashioned and pretty look.

Many bridal gloves were fingerless mitts to accom-modate slipping the wedding ring on the ring finger without the bride having to remove her glove. LaCrasia has a glove specially made for them in China that is a delicately crocheted nylon glove, wrist-length. The unusual feature is that the wedding-ring finger is left off. The gloves have a sweetly fragile air, and one size fits all. Available for $15.00 postpaid from the address above. Ask for the Bridal Gloves.

The Wedding Cake

Along with the flowers, the wedding cake is often not given the attention it deserves. It can make a very dramatic presentation, and it ought to taste better than it often does at wedding receptions.

As to what the cake will be made of, tradition allows a large choice. Richard J. Hooker tells us that often "a pound cake was used for weddings, though by the late 1850s the lady cake, which was a white cake, and plum cake were becoming more common." The development of baking powder and baking soda allowed cakes to become lighter in texture. Hooker also traces the tradition of giving the wedding guest a piece of cake to take home (and put under a young lady's pillow) to New England around this time. In New England mixtures of fruit, nuts, and spices were mixed with molasses for a "black cake."

Victorian cakes were considerably richer than what we are used to now. Jill Gardner in *Victorian Cakes* tells us that we would find them heavy, for "the buttery, eggy, milky quality of their crumb attests to the good honest ingredients they contain." The flour available was generally bread flour. For cakes, bakers used flour mixed with cornstarch to give a lighter texture. Sugar crystals were much coarser and so a greater amount of sugar was required for both sweetening and to dissolve the gluten in the flour. The amount of sugar used in the nineteenth century would likely be too much for our palate today. Also today's lard (if we wanted to use it!) is quite different as is the blander flavor of modern currants and raisins. As can be imagined, almost every ingredient that was used is quite different, thus making old recipes very difficult to duplicate. An 1860 recipe in *Godey's Lady's Book* for a Rich Bride's Cake or Christening Cake calls for five pounds of "the finest flour dried and sifted," five pounds of "picked and washed currants dried before the fire," and three

pounds of butter, two pounds of "loaf sugar," sixteen eggs, numerous spices, a gill of mountain wine, and a gill of brandy. As cake pans were not yet known the baker was advised to use a hoop lined with paper and well-rubbed with butter. Bake ovens became more modern after the 1870s, and cake pans came into use, so cakes began to take on the shapes and textures we are more familiar with today. The standard groom's cake, however, would be dense and textured, probably like a fruit cake. The wedding cake was and is a multitiered, white, and lovely creation.

All of the above really means that today you can feel free to select the kind or kinds of cake you like and have just a wedding cake or the additional bride's and groom's cakes as well. Because the wedding cake was symbolically so important, it generally was placed on a table of its own.

A wedding cake may be decorated with real flowers. There is a tradition for doing this, and it is the simplest way to carry out a floral theme in lieu of a really excellent baker who can make sugar flowers. Never stick the flowers directly into the cake without a holder of some kind. Flowers are not grown under the same pesticide restrictions as vegetables and fruit. Plastic cups containing Oasis™, a substance that holds moisture, are available from florists. You insert the stems in the cup containing the dampened Oasis™, and then the cup is placed in the cake. When cutting the cake, you can remove the whole cup with the flowers making the process much less messy. Remember also that real flowers will not hold up very long. An alternative is to use silk flowers. Be careful when buying silk flowers, however, as many of the colors are not true to life.

So the essence of the Victorian style is to make the

*Wedding cake created
by Sylvia Weinstock.*

*Wedding cake created
by Sylvia Weinstock.*

wedding cake look as romantic and decorative as possible and to present it dramatically. A few prominent custom cakemakers are featured below.

Sylvia Weinstock
273 Church Street
New York, New York 10013
(212) 925-6698

If Sylvia Weinstock had been baking in the Victorian era, she would have made the cakes for Society's weddings just as she does today. She creates cakes for the well-known and for those others who give the wedding cake the thought and place it deserves at a wedding reception. Every album includes a picture of the cake being cut by the bride and groom.

Sylvia so far makes few Victorian cake replicas. However, she can actually create almost anything in cake form. Some of the cakes she has made are not only wonderfully romantic but quite intricate. For example, one was topped with a rustic cabin for a couple who met hiking, and another with a lovely sand castle for a couple who met at the beach. Sylvia could certainly create a Victorian-style cake from a drawing or a good description. In the romantic spirit of the Victorian era, she can create something that is of special meaning to the prospective bride and groom who are steeped in Victoriana. But many of her floral creations are already quite close to the nineteenth-century ideal because the wedding cake has really changed very little during the last century.

The flowers on Sylvia's cakes are handmade out of sugar to match the flowers of the bridal bouquet, those on the bridal gown, or the floral centerpieces at the reception. It is difficult to differentiate between Sylvia's sugar flowers on the cake and the real flowers at the party.

Sylvia feels that not enough attention is given to the height of the cake in relation to the height of the room, and Victorian wedding cakes always had height. However, the height of the cake should be kept in proportion to the room. In other words, if you need a fairly large cake but have ordinary ceiling height, plan to make a wider cake. If you have a very tall ceiling use a narrower cake, but make it taller. The cake should be seen from all parts of the room, but it should not appear to be too tall.

Because she is both an artist and a baker, Sylvia consults with the bride to design the cake that she will then create for the wedding. Directions for cutting the cake are always included. Sylvia does need quite a bit of advance notice (about two months for the busy spring and fall wedding seasons). The tops of her cakes are intended to be kept as keepsakes. She has often duplicated the centerpiece from the mother-of-the-bride's cake, and re-creates original cakes for anniversary celebrations.

In an interview with this wonderful baker, Sylvia provided some remarks about receptions and cakes in general, which while not strictly for a Victorian-style wedding, are helpful for any wedding planner.

The kind of cake you have depends on the season and the number of people it must serve. For instance a Dacquoise (a meringue) would not be good for three hundred people, so a type that works well in large size should be chosen. The size of the cake dictates what it will be made of. Chocolate, for instance, is a firm cake that can be made in large sizes just as were the fruit cakes in the Victorian era. A cheesecake may be iced with a white icing to give an old-fashioned look. However, cheesecake

For the bride who prefers a traditional wedding cake, Margaret Lastick can design a classically romantic one all in white. (Photograph by Robert Lastick)

• 123 •

The Victorians had a bride's cake at the wedding and at each anniversary afterwards. Traditionally, it was a round white cake. Margaret Lastick embellishes hers with flowers made of gum paste combined with real flowers. (Photograph by Robert Lastick)

Margaret Lastick sometimes combines real flowers with sugar flowers when designing a wedding cake, as can be seen in this elegant example of her art. (Photograph by Robert Lastick)

In this romantic wedding cake Margaret Lastick uses lilies of the valley, a favorite flower of Victorian brides. The bride and groom, on their very own music box, dance the first waltz in a pavillon d'amour, which is created with porcelain pillars and a styrofoam top and lavishly covered with lilies of the valley. The entire top is made on a separate base so that it can be removed from the cake and placed under a glass dome in order to grace the anniversary cakes to come. (Photograph by Robert Lastick)

This cake was created for a garden wedding by Cile Bellefleur-Burbidge.

must be cut with a hot knife. Sylvia likes a cake to be seasonal. For instance, for a summer wedding you might want a fresh, lemony cake or perhaps a mousse.

Here are some general suggestions that Sylvia has for wedding receptions. Keep the reception relatively simple, providing just white wine and champagne for example. Don't rent champagne glasses, buy inexpensive ones. Thus you can give some of the glasses away as mementos to the bridesmaids, and the remainder can be used for your next party.

Margaret Lastick
Le Royale Icing, Inc.
329 South Ridgeland Ave.
Oak Park, Illinois 60302
(708) 386-4175

Margaret Lastick believes that the wedding cake is as important as the gown the bride will wear on her wedding day, and considers every detail of the wedding, including the colors, the season, the room, the style of the bride's gown, the flowers, and even the favorite cake flavors of the bride and groom before she designs a cake.

Each of her cakes is custom made and, no matter where the wedding will take place, Margaret escorts her cake to its final destination to assemble it and put on the final touches. She and her cakes have been known to fly first class from her headquarters in Oak Park, Illinois, to many different points in the United States. They are never shipped.

Although Margaret describes herself as a pastry chef, both *Bon Appetit* and *Victoria* magazines have stated that she is one of the best custom-cake creators. Flowers such as stephanotis, tiger lilies, sweet peas, roses, tulips, and orchids—just to name a few—are modeled one petal at a time. Decorations, such as swans, are made from pulled-sugar ribbons, an almost lost art. All are edible.

The cake, itself, is just as elegant as the decorations. Some of the combinations she uses are butter sponge cake, laced with Fra Angelico and layered with cinnamon-hazelnut buttercream; chocolate sponge cake laced with Grand Marnier and layered with Belgian-chocolate ganache and French-chocolate buttercream;

and yellow cake with New York cheesecake and caramel-walnut filling.

Her office is in her home and her kitchen is in Chicago, Illinois, where she handles as many as eight weddings a week with the help of five pastry chefs.

In addition to cakes for weddings, she has created wedding cakes for Tiffany & Co.'s windows in Chicago.

Cile Bellefleur-Burbidge
12 Stafford Road
Danvers, Massachusetts 01923-2439
(508) 774-3514

The inspiration for much of Cile Bellefleur-Burbidge's wedding cakes comes from the opulence of the Victorian era. She believes the greatest compliment that can be paid to her edible masterpieces is their complete disappearance. "Their fate is similar to a gorgeous display of fireworks—marveled at for a moment and then gone forever—but such a lovely moment."

John Loring in his book *The Tiffany Wedding* wrote that "Cile Bellefleur-Burbidge brings the art of cake decoration to a level of elegance and sophistication that recalls the dazzling Dresden centerpieces made for European royalty."

A Victorian Fan cake made by Cile Bellefleur-Burbidge.

Wedding cake called "Victorian Fantasy in Pink and White" made by Cile Belle-fleur-Burbidge.

Here is an all-white version of the "Victorian Fantasy" cake. Photograph © 1991 by Miller Studio Photographers.

The cake she created for her daughter's wedding in 1990, which she calls "Victorian Fantasy in Pink and White," is typical of the elaborate and elegant forms for which she is so well known. It stood three feet tall. The base comprised eight projecting cakes (four of chocolate and four of carrot) each framed in delicate lattice work and overlaid with royal-icing drapery swags, and a profusion of pink and mauve royal-icing flowers. The second layer (pound cake with raspberry filling) featured eight more lattice panels interspersed by small panels appliquéd with sugar cherubs. The third section (created over a styrofoam base as further cake was not needed) was an octagonal shape paneled in lattice work. S-shaped scrolls of royal icing projected from the panels sweeping upward to support an overhanging "terrace." Centered between the scrolls were sugar urns filled with flowers. Overhead drapery swags hung in midair attached to the scrolls by icing bows. The cake was then topped with an urn of solid sugar filled with hundreds of royal icing flowers in pink and mauve. What is especially delightful about this is that the entire basket of flowers can be removed from the top and displayed under a glass dome for many years as a romantic remembrance of a very special day.

She has created the same design all in white for the bride who prefers a traditional wedding cake.

Still another cake Cile designed and made for a garden wedding was decorated with royal-icing flowers to repeat the colors of the real flowers in the garden.

Her Victorian Fan Cake, which was one of a series created for Tiffany & Co.'s windows in New York, has also been used as the focal point for a small wedding with a Victorian theme.

Beneath all the decorative splendor of Cile's cakes, there are delicious combinations of natural-food compounds: chocolate or pound cake, buttercream frosting, and even a fruitcake saturated with brandy and with an apricot purée covering and sheets of marzipan paste. Cile Bellefleur-Burbidge's cakes entrance the palate as well as astonish the eye.

Here are some additional cakemakers that you should know about.

Betty Van Nostrand
6 Leonard Road
Poughkeepsie, New York 12601
(914) 471-3386

Betty Van Nostrand's specialty is making spun-sugar "lace" icing that matches the lace on the bridal gown.

The Cake Shoppe's Bridal Suite
Barbara J. McCann
116 W. Chicago Boulevard
Tecumseh, Michigan 49286
1-800-525-1165 or (517) 423-7733

The Cake Shoppe has adapted the traditional Victorian wedding cake (a fruit cake) to a softer, moist cake, which makes it possible for The Cake Shoppe to offer an elaborate Victorian-style wedding cake that has a taste and texture more to modern tastes. The elaborate Victorian icing techniques are accomplished with buttercream icing rather than the hard royal icing used in Victorian days. The several designs available should satisfy the desire for a cake that looks really Victorian but tastes the way we want it to today. Call the wedding consultant and ask about the V1850 series of Victorian wedding cakes.

The cake provided for our wedding breakfast at The Hermitage was baked by Susan Lang Simon. You can reach her at (212) 489-5203.

Where to Have the Wedding

Where to have the wedding is the first decision to make after the number of wedding guests has been settled. As a matter of fact, in some cases it may be the first decision, for if you fall in love with a place that is a bit out of the way, you will probably have to pare down the guest list. Many historic houses or museums are situated in historic areas and have wonderful bed & breakfast inns nearby to house guests overnight. Having the ceremony and reception in a smaller place such as a small historic house or a bed & breakfast inn is often a good excuse to think carefully about how many guests you will want to invite. On the other hand, if you pick a big mansion or a ballroom, you might want to have a larger wedding than you had originally planned. The time of year is probably one of the most important determining factors for your plans, as many of the most beautiful historic houses and small hotels only allow weddings during their off seasons.

One couple that shared their wedding plans with us said that they picked the date for the wedding re-creation from the date of the house they were getting married in. So for a period wedding, the house itself may be an inspiration as to how formal the wedding will be, the style of the wedding dress, and the refreshments.

Here in New York you can get married in romantic spots like the Boathouse in Central Park or the Picnic House in Prospect Park, Brooklyn. The New York Botanical Garden in the Bronx and the Brooklyn Botanic Garden offer indoor/outdoor wedding sites. Most cities, large or small, have similar sites that are available. With the interest in historic preservation growing around the country, it is not unusual to find that a small town has a gazebo or a common that makes a wonderful setting for a ceremony. There are also yachts and ferries for rent,

and other vehicles such steamboats, trains, and trolleys. These are often not places immediately thought of, which makes them even more interesting. If you don't know of any interesting sites, just search out a museum or historic house and call them and ask for a referral if that place is not for you or does not host weddings. The ordinary glitzy catering hall is generally the very antithesis of what a Victorian wedding was all about, so it is worth giving the setting for your wedding a great deal of attention at the very beginning of your planning efforts.

HISTORIC SITES

The following is a list of historic sites that we know may be rented for weddings because they have confirmed the fact to us. It is intended to show the variety of settings available and to inspire the prospective couple to search out these wonderful museums, historic houses, and buildings in their own areas. For the Victorian-style wedding, there is really nothing more wonderful than a beautiful Victorian house, and many of these houses provide a sense of opulence and charm that cannot be matched.

It is often difficult to tell how many guests may be accommodated in a historic site, for some places will let you use the whole house, while others only offer a room or two, although that may be a ballroom. Many allow weddings only during certain months or seasons. There may also be several restrictions when renting a historic site because they are under the auspices of state governments, museum boards, or preservation societies.

We have included restrictions if they were reported to us, but it is always best to call well in advance and check on the guidelines, as they may affect your decision even if you love the house. Here are some of the most frequent restrictions: you must use a caterer approved by the historic site (on the other hand, many houses or museums give you free rein in the field of food and beverages); no alcohol is allowed; or only the grounds may be available. Some sites offer tents, tables, and even linen, and let you have your own caterer. You will soon discover that there are wide differences among the rules at each site, so be sure to check.

If you know of a historic house that is not listed here, by all means call and see if they do allow weddings. Some are just beginning to, as it is a fairly new idea. Often, if weddings are not allowed at that particular place, the person you contact may be able to tell you about one that does have weddings, perhaps one you are unfamiliar with. Those in the business of running historic sites can suggest more and better possibilities than any outsider.

ARKANSAS

Villa Marre
Dorthey Dutton, Coordinator
Quapaw Quarter Association
P.O. Box 1104
Little Rock, Arkansas 72203
(501) 371-0075

The Villa Marre is a beautifully restored Second Empire mansion on Scott Street in Little Rock, now owned and operated by Little Rock's historic preservation organization. The house has stenciled ceilings, parquet floors, crystal chandeliers, and ornate furnishings that recall the gracious elegance of the turn of the century.

CALIFORNIA

Ralston Hall/College of Notre Dame
Peggy Hart, Coordinator
1500 Ralston Avenue
Belmont, California 94002
(415) 593-1601, ext. 201

Ralston Hall is the center of the campus of the College of Notre Dame, situated in the ruggedly beautiful and

Villa Marre, Little Rock, Arkansas

secluded Canada del Diablo, twenty-one miles south of San Francisco. The core of the house is an 1850 villa over which William Chapman Ralston, a financier and founder of the Bank of California, created a Victorian mansion with over eighty rooms in the Italian-villa style. The huge ground floor of Ralston Hall is available for wedding receptions.

Fischer-Hanlon House and Garden, Benicia, California

Fischer-Hanlon House and Garden
Benicia Capitol State Historic Park
P.O. Box 5
Benicia, California 94510
(707) 745-3385

This very early pioneer building, in a style more often found in New England, was converted to a home in 1858 by Joseph Fischer for his Irish bride. It has a lovely old-fashioned garden that is one of the few remaining original gardens in the state. It is available for wedding parties for up to one hundred people.

Kohl Mansion
Pat Nelson
2750 Adeline Drive
Burlingame, California 94010
(415) 343-3631

The Kohl Mansion was built in 1914 on forty acres of oak-covered hillside. The elegant, rosebrick Tudor mansion has an Elizabethan–style Great Hall, Clock Hall, Morning Room, Dining Room and Library for receptions. Part of the house may be rented for a wedding, or the whole house so that parties from large to small will find appropriate settings. There is also a large swimming pool, three tennis courts, and a large lawn area that may also be part of the wedding.

Homestead Museum
Max A. van Balgooy
15415 East Don Julian Road
City of Industry, California 91745-1029
(818) 968-8492

This six-acre site documents ninety years of California history. The Workman House is an 1840 adobe that was remodeled in the 1870s. La Casa Nueva was built in the 1920s. Wedding receptions for up to 250 seated guests can be held on the lawn in the shadow of the 1920 mansion, surrounded by the beautiful palm trees and other exotic plants in the garden. Smaller receptions can be held in the Victorian Workman house.

Camron-Stanford House, Oakland, California

Camron-Stanford House
Liz Way
1418 Lakeside Drive
Oakland, California 94612
(510) 836-1976

The Camron-Stanford House is an 1876 house museum on the shore of Lake Merritt. More than 100 people can be accommodated for a wedding reception. The House had a wedding in 1877 that is well documented and provides inspiration for many couples.

Rockefeller Lodge—Partytime Catering
Joyce and Deborah Wilson
2650 Market Street
Richmond/San Pablo, California 94806
(510) 235-7344

This is an inn where catering is the specialty. The historic house was once John D. Rockefeller's west-coast retreat and hunting lodge. There is an elegant dining room with a huge fireplace, and the grounds have hundred-year-old brick walks, spacious lawns, and more than 150 species of exotic plants. Wedding arrangements range from picnics to banquets and include invitations and accessories.

Hamlin Mansion
Donna Balsamo
2120 Broadway
San Francisco, California 94115
(415) 331-0544

The impressive Hamlin Mansion features an elegant and spacious foyer, as well as the great hall complete with ornate oak columns, and a two-story space crowned by a leaded-glass skylight. The magnificent staircase is perfect for presenting the bride. The dining room has a gold and black marble fireplace and great views of San Francisco bay. The mansion can hold up to 200 seated guests and a standing capacity of 350.

Whittier Mansion
2090 Jackson Street
San Francisco, California 94109-2896
(415) 567-1849

This beautiful thirty-one-room Pacific Heights mansion was built in 1896 by William Franklin Whittier. It is now owned and managed by the California Historical Society. The mansion is the epitome of the grand and gracious scale of living around the turn of the century in San Francisco. It has huge hand-carved fireplaces, imported marble, mahogany and white-oak woodwork, rich oriental rugs, and opulent furnishings. The whole mansion is available for weddings up to 350 guests, and smaller numbers can be accommodated by using just one of the three floors. The main floor's living and dining rooms are perfect for a dinner with up to 150 guests. The Whittier ballroom is available for dancing.

Villa Montalvo
Contact: Judy Carollo
15400 Montalvo Road
Saratoga, California 95071
(408) 741-3421

This Mediterranean-style villa was built in 1912 for the mayor of San Francisco (later senator from California) and was named for a sixteenth-century Spanish writer, García Ordóñez de Montalvo. In one of his tales he describes an island rich with gold and jewels and called his fantasy island "California," providing inspiration for the name of the state. The villa has a spread of 175 acres and is twenty minutes from downtown San Jose.

Weddings at Montalvo are held in the Oval Garden, a formal English garden, from May through mid-September, or in the villa itself. Champagne and cake, and small receptions are permitted after the ceremony and the garden can accommodate up to 200 guests. Floral arrangements, music, and photographers' services may be contracted for directly, or though the villa. Because of the special nature of the facilities, however, any food or beverage arrangements may only be made through the villa's preferred caterers.

CONNECTICUT

Bowen House
("Roseland Cottage")
Charlene W. Perkins
P.O. Box 186
Woodstock, Connecticut 06281
(203) 928-4074

Built in 1846 as a summer home, Roseland is a lovely Gothic Revival house painted bright pink and richly ornamented. The cottage contains its original Gothic Revival furniture and has an indoor bowling alley, believed to be the oldest in the country. This property is owned by the Society for The Preservation of New England Antiquities (SPNEA). The lovely grounds feature a Victorian parterre garden outlined with 600 yards of boxwood hedging and has thousands of flowers. The carriage house can accommodate 150 people, and with the use of a tent 300 guests can be accommodated. Famous as a site for lavish celebrations in the nineteenth century, Roseland still provides a gracious setting for an indoor or outdoor wedding.

ILLINOIS

Beverly Unitarian Church
Dr. Roger A. Brewin, Minister
10244 South Longwood Drive

Chicago, Illinois 60643
(312) 233-7080

The church is a replica of a seventeenth-century baronial castle that was built around 1886. The interior features restored golden-oak woodwork, handcarved doors and seven small stained-glass panels, including a beautiful 1886 family-dedication window. The overall effect is one of simplified elegance. The church is located in the Beverly Hills/Morgan Park area, the largest Urban Historic District in the nation with over three thousand homes listed on the National Register. Up to 125 guests can be accommodated for a wedding ceremony and reception, and the church also hosts rehearsal dinners and showers. The Beverly Unitarian Church has hosted many theme weddings including Victorian, and Dr. Brewin has a turn-of-the-century street-preaching frock coat and plumed hat for such occasions. Couples with imaginative plans are welcomed, and there are no restrictions regarding membership in the church or for any other reason. The only requirement is that couples meet twice with the minister to plan their own ceremony. For ceremonies or receptions with larger guest lists, the church has access to other sanctuaries and halls in the immediate neighborhood. Dr. Brewin will also travel to other locations in the Chicago area to perform

ceremonies. Parties and ceremonies are also popular for the renewal of vows on wedding anniversaries. The church has a catering service, or you may provide your own.

INDIANA

Morris-Butler House Museum
Tiffany C. Sallee, Administrator
1204 North Park Avenue
Indianapolis, Indiana 46202
(317) 636-5409

This magnificent Second Empire–style mansion, owned by the Historic Landmarks Foundation of Indiana, echoes the rich ambiance of Victorian life in Indianapolis at its most opulent. This is a unique place for a sit-down dinner or an elegant buffet because the dining room may be used

Beverly Unitarian Church, Chicago, Illinois

Morris-Butler House Museum, Indianapolis, Indiana

for up to eighteen guests. Landmark Dining re-creates an authentic nineteenth-century dinner experience from soup to demitasse and brandy. For larger warm-weather receptions, the courtyard and and garden directly behind the House will hold up to 250 guests.

IOWA

Liberty Hall Historic Center
1300 West Main Street
Lamoni, Iowa 50140
(515) 784-6133

Liberty Hall is a historic house museum that originally belonged to the family of Joseph Smith III, who was the first president of the Reorganized Church of Jesus Christ of Latter Day Saints. The eighteen-room farmhouse is on the National Register and can accommodate a wedding ceremony and a small reception, as well as a luncheon or lawn picnic.

Mathias Ham House
Historic Site at Eagle Point
P.O. Box 305
Dubuque, Iowa 52001
(319) 557-9545

The stately 1857 home of Mathias Ham (one of the first settlers to cross the Mississippi River into Iowa) is a distinctive example of the Italian-villa style of architecture. It is situated at Eagle Point, overlooking the Mississippi River, in the port of Dubuque, which includes the Woodward Riverboat Museum, a sidewheeler steamboat, and the National Rivers Hall of Fame. The villa has thirteen-feet-high ceilings, gilt moldings, and evokes the life during Dubuque's colorful pre–Civil War steamboat era. The Mathias Ham House's summer kitchen (three rooms) accommodates fifty-two people. This facility works well for rehearsal dinners or small wedding parties. Food service can be arranged with the caterer of the wedding consultant or with the bride's caterer. A progressive dinner with live music accommodates groups of fifteen or more. There are options of music and carriage rides (Colleen's Carriage Rides, (319) 556-6431 or trolley rides for the wedding party.

MASSACHUSETTS

Lyman Estate
(known as "The Vale")
185 Lyman Street
Waltham, Massachusetts 02154
(617) 893-7232

The original house on the Lyman Estate was designed in 1793 by famed Salem architect Samuel McIntire. The house was subsequently enlarged and remodeled in the 1880s, and then again in 1912. The result is a remarkably handsome mansion in the Colonial Revival style. The ballroom and parlor retain their Federal design created in the late eighteenth century. The Vale is admired for its landscaped gardens, the greenhouses that include early examples of solar construction, and the prize-winning camellia trees and Black Hamburg grapevines from Hampton Court in England. The Vale is owned and operated by the Society for the Preservation of New England Antiquities (SPNEA), and although it is not a Victorian house, it is an unusually lovely setting for a wedding.

Lyman Estate ("The Vale"), Waltham, Massachusetts

Martha-Mary Chapel, Dearborn, Michigan

MICHIGAN

Martha-Mary Chapel
Henry Ford Museum & Greenfield Village
Anne McIntosh
P.O. Box 1970
Dearborn, Michigan 48121
(313) 271-1620

On the grounds of this twelve-acre indoor/outdoor historic complex is the early Victorian Martha-Mary Chapel, where over 200 weddings a year are still performed. There are facilities, including catering, available for a wedding reception as well.

MISSOURI

Missouri Town 1855
Susan Burton
Heritage Programs & Museums
Independence Square Courthouse

Suite 205
Independence, Missouri 64050
(816) 881-4431

Missouri Town 1855 is a national historic site comprising many historic buildings, including Fort Osage and the Harry S. Truman Courtroom and Office. The church is a hewn-log structure built in 1844 and may be rented for the ceremony; it accommodates about 100 people. The Fleming Park Meeting Hall at Lake Jacomo is available for the reception. What makes this a really unusual wedding experience is the variety of options that can go along with the reception, including a hayride, buggy rides, bonfires, picnic lunches, or hearth-cooked dinners.

The Hermitage, Ho-Ho-Kus, New Jersey

NEW JERSEY

The Hermitage
Florence Leon
335 Franklin Turnpike
Ho-Ho-Kus, New Jersey 07423
(201) 445-8311

This lovely Gothic Revival house, a National Landmark, is the site of the wedding breakfast illustrated in this book. Wedding receptions may be held for up to 175 guests, using both the interior and exterior, including the verandah and tents.

NEW YORK

The Octagon House
(The Armor-Stiner House)
Joseph Pell Lombardi
45 West Clinton Avenue
Irvington-on-Hudson, New York 10533
(212) 349-0700

This unique octagonal Victorian house has been lovingly restored by architect Joseph Pell Lombardi. It has a wonderful octagonal ballroom in the top story and a lovely wraparound verandah. It is available for wedding parties. Situated in a lovely rural setting, the Octagon House is a magnificent example of Victorian architecture.

Old Merchant's House
Pi Gardner, Director
29 East Fourth Street
New York, New York 10003
(212) 777-1089

Old Merchant's House, New York, New York (Photograph by John Kosmer)

This beautifully restored Greek Revival townhouse is one of the last vestiges of Old New York. Small wedding parties may be accommodated for a marriage ceremony and reception in the parlor and dining room, and there is a family parlor downstairs. The Treadwell Mansion (as it is also called) will be closed for part of 1992 for restoration, but reservations can be made for afterwards.

The Casino in Congress Park, Saratoga Springs, New York

The Casino in Congress Park
Contact: Mary Zabala
City Hall
5 Lake Avenue
Saratoga Springs, New York 12866
(518) 587-3550

The Casino, as it is simply known now, is a beautiful three-story Italianate building situated in thirty-three-acre Congress Park, which is in the center of Saratoga Springs. The main building was built by John Morrissey in 1870. The beautiful Victorian-era parlor is used for weddings, and there is also a bar area. The most unusual feature is the lovely ballroom, which is the 1902 addition designed by Canfield. Formerly known as Canfield Casino, this is where society gambled in the opulent era of Saratoga Springs. It has octagon-shaped stained-glass windows in the ceiling which have been beautifully restored. The parlor, bar area, and the ballroom can accommodate from 300 to 400 guests. This is a superb setting for a wedding ceremony and reception, but there is at least a year's wait to reserve a date.

Perfect Parties at Snug Harbor
Carol Kelly
1000 Richmond Terrace
Staten Island, New York 10301
(718) 816-0011

• 139 •

Snug Harbor is a large collection of historic buildings, including museums, botanical gardens, and a music hall. Perfect Parties is the part of the organization that will help you with your wedding plans. The Governor's House, a nineteenth-century home on beautifully landscaped grounds, provides an elegant, intimate setting for up to thirty-two for a seated dinner and seventy-five for a buffet. The Great Hall, a magnificent Beaux Arts building with thirty-five-foot ceilings, can accommodate up to 500 for buffet-style parties and 350 for a sit-down dinner. The parkland is also available for tented parties. There are two delightful trolleys that can be rented; "Suzy" has a tape deck and "Jack" also has heat and air-conditioning.

Lyndhurst, Tarrytown, New York

Lyndhurst
Sheila Halpern
635 South Broadway
Tarrytown, New York 10591
(914) 631-0046

This wonderful Gothic Revival mansion is owned and operated by the National Trust for Historic Preservation. Ceremonies and receptions are allowed only outdoors on the sixty-seven landscaped acres along the Hudson River that surround the house. Weddings can be held in the evenings, from 5:30 p.m. to 10:30 p.m. in late May, June, August, and September. The receptions are held in a tent on the lawn and valet and field parking is available. The Verandah and Rose Garden are available for the cocktail hour and wedding ceremony respectively, and a tour of the mansion can be arranged during the cocktail hour. Lyndhurst superbly embodies the opulence of the Victorian era.

OHIO

Piatt Castles
Elizabeth Marshall
10051 Township Road 47

Castle Piatt Mac-A-Cheek, West Liberty, Ohio

West Liberty, Ohio 43357
(513) 465-2821

Castle Piatt Mac-A-Cheek is a Norman-French-style chateau that was built around 1864. A thirty-two-room limestone mansion, it contains some antique furniture, and there is even a private chapel. Castle Piatt Mac-O-Chee, built about 1879 in the style of a Flemish chateau, was extravagantly decorated and frescoed by the French artist Oliver Frey. Mac-O-Chee contains a collection of tapestries, art objects, and furniture ranging from 150 to 800 years old. The Piatt family came to North America from Dauphine in southern France 300 years ago, when the Mack ack ocheek towns were a Shawnee stronghold. The Castles are situated on lovely grounds in rural Logan County.

RHODE ISLAND

Blithewold Gardens & Arboretum
Contact: Harriet Linn
101 Ferry Road
Bristol, Rhode Island 02809-0417
(401) 253-2707

Formerly the summer home of a Pennsylvania coal baron, Blithewold is a forty-five-room, elegant turn-of-the-century mansion surrounded by thirty-three acres of landscaped grounds, all overlooking Narragansett Bay. The house was originally built in 1890 as a summer residence to serve as a place to anchor the magnificent yacht that Mr. Van Winkle had purchased as a birthday gift for his wife. A model of the yacht is on display in the mansion. The property, owned by the Heritage Trust of Rhode Island, is available for wedding receptions after 4:30 p.m. from April through October. The first floor of the mansion, a space that includes two covered porches and a terrace, will accommodate up to 100 people. To accommodate groups of more than 100 people a tent must be rented and set up on Blithewold's Great Lawn at the rear of the mansion, with some limited use of the mansion permitted. There are kitchen facilities for caterers. The house has a fully furnished dressing room for the bride on the second floor, and there is a grand

Blithewold Gardens & Aroboretum, Bristol, Rhode Island

staircase for the bride to descend on her way to the altar. Blithewold's North Garden, with its lush perennial borders, provides a lovely, natural setting for outdoor wedding ceremonies.

Commodore Edgar Mansion, Portsmouth, Rhode Island

Commodore Edgar Mansion
Cheryl Hackett-Galvin
25 Old Beach Road
P.O. Box 285
Portsmouth, Rhode Island 02840
(401) 683-6923

This Gilded Age mansion was designed in 1861 by the famed New York architectural firm of McKim, Mead, and White. It incorporates the grand architectural styles of Rosecliff, Kingscote, and the Newport Casino in nearby Newport. The lush gardens can be seen through the first sliding glass windows used in the United States, and the handcarved stone fireplace and other appointments are in the opulent Newport style. The mansion has a ballroom and can accommodate weddings of all sizes.

Rosecliff
The Preservation Society of Newport County
Philip Pelletier
118 Mill Street
Newport, Rhode Island 02840
(401) 847-1000

Rosecliff, one of the great Newport mansions, is on Bellevue Avenue. It was built in 1902 and designed by Stanford White in a style inspired by the Grand Trianon at Versailles. This handsome mansion was the scene of many brilliant entertainments in its day. It is now so popular for wedding receptions that you need to book at least a year in advance.

TEXAS

Ashton Villa
Barbara Lawrence
2328 Broadway
Galveston, Texas 77550
(409) 762-3933

An elegant 1859 mansion, Ashton Villa provides an enchanting setting for weddings and receptions. The ballroom has been the site of some of Galveston Island's grandest affairs. There is a caterer's kitchen and

Ashton Villa, Galveston, Texas

convenient parking. Three hundred guests may be accommodated for stand-up functions; 200 to 225 for seated dinners. Brides may also use the house for wedding photographs even if not renting the ballroom.

Elissa: An 1877 Tall Ship
Patti Bellis
Pier 21
Galveston, Texas 77550
(409) 765-1877

The restored 1877 tall ship *Elissa* and adjacent pier are a favorite site for couples who want a unique romantic ambiance. With the moon peeking through the towering masts and stars twinkling over the water, an *Elissa* wedding or reception is sure to be memorable. Up to 500 guests can be accommodated on the *Elissa* and at dockside. The *Elissa* is available only after regular visiting hours. Rental includes the decks, the hold below, the galley for use as a serving area, and the captain's quarters. The dock will accommodate 300 for seated dinner parties.

St. Joseph's Church
Galveston Historical Foundation
22nd Street and Avenue K
Galveston, Texas 77550
(409) 765-7834

Elissa: An 1877 Tall Ship, Galveston, Texas

The first German Catholic Church in Texas, this charming 1859 wooden-frame structure features a coffered ceiling decorated in delicate, hand-painted hues. This is a charming early Victorian setting for a ceremony.

Samuel May Williams Home
Frank Correia
3601 Avenue P
Galveston, Texas 77550
(409) 765-1839

St. Joseph's Church, Galveston, Texas

One of the two oldest houses on Galveston Island, the Williams Home, built in 1839, offers an intimate setting for small weddings and receptions. The verandah and spacious lawn may be used for outdoor weddings for 125 to 150 guests, and the interior is available for smaller groups of about twenty-five.

VIRGINIA

Maymont
Patricia Denny, Director of Community Development
c/o Maymont Foundation
1700 Hampton Street

Samuel May Williams Home, Galveston, Texas

Maymont, Richmond, Virginia

Richmond, Virginia 23220
(804) 358-7166

Maymont is a turn-of-the-century estate of more than 100 acres with several beautiful gardens that are ideal settings for outdoor weddings. The formal Italian Rose Garden is the most popular setting for outdoor weddings. There is an indoor/outdoor reception area, and there are wedding-carriage rides. Maymont can accommodate a maximum of 150 people for a wedding or a reception.

BED & BREAKFAST INNS, SMALL HOTELS

Most Victorian weddings were held at home—sometimes both the ceremony and the reception, but, generally, after a church ceremony the home was the most popular place for the wedding breakfast. Today, however, a home that can accommodate a wedding reception is unusual. A satisfying alternative is the homelike atmosphere of a bed & breakfast inn. Therefore, we are providing below a list of some bed & breakfast inns around the country that have made a specialty of having weddings in their establishments. If we haven't listed one in your area, look through some of the publications listed in the back of this book for ideas about more B&B's that may host wedding ceremonies and receptions. Also, don't hesitate to call a B&B you have heard of or have passed on the road, for they might be interested in the project even if they haven't thought of it before. After all, the whole bed & breakfast concept just began to take hold in this country in the 1980s, and more innkeepers are setting up all the time. One drawback to the bed & breakfast inn is that they are generally small in size and cannot accommodate large receptions. There are exceptions, of course, and in good weather or in the West and South the outdoors can add to the number of guests that may be accommodated. We have also listed some restored hotels and large inns for the larger reception. What is not to be found on the list are buildings that are Victorian or turn of the century, but are not period restorations inside. There are many such in all parts of the country, but they do not meet our criteria for recommendation. If that is all that is available, however, the flowers and food will help to re-create the ambiance. Many of these buildings are historic and are on the National Register of Historic Places, but they have been separated from the list of Historic Sites because they are privately owned and operated.

ARKANSAS

The Queen Anne Mansion
Ron or Mary Lou Evans
207 Kings Highway
Eureka Springs, Arkansas 72632
(501) 253-8825

This beautiful mansion was originally built in 1891 in Carthage, Missouri. In 1984 it was disassembled, moved, and rebuilt in Eureka Springs. The house has been meticulously restored with its beautiful woodwork, stained-glass windows, and antique lighting. Wedding receptions and ceremonies of up to 400 people can be accommodated.

Patton House B&B Inn
Mary Lee Shirley
P.O. Box 61
Wooster, Arkansas 72181

A country setting with a special gazebo for outdoor ceremonies.

CALIFORNIA

Garratt Mansion
900 Union Street
Alameda, California 94501
(415) 521-4779

This large turn-of-the-century house may be rented for weddings of up to 120 guests during the winter and 150 in nice weather when the porch, balcony, and gardens can be used. There is also room for dancing.

Carter House Country Inn, Eureka, California (Photograph by Patrick Cudahy)

Carter House Country Inn
Mark and Christi Carter
1033 Third Street
Eureka, California 95501
(707) 445-1390

This handsome Victorian mansion was reproduced from hundred-year-old architectural plans in 1982. The original plans had been used to build an 1884 house destroyed by the 1906 earthquake and fire. The present re-creation is on a hillside in Eureka with views of the bay and of the nearby Carson Mansion, one of the most unusual examples of Victorian architecture in the country. The Carter House is elegantly furnished and has an excellent restaurant. They can accommodate ceremonies and receptions for fifty to seventy-five people.

Hotel Carter
Mark Carter
301 L Street
Eureka, California 95501
(707) 445-8062

The Carters built this Victorian hotel across the street from their inn listed above. The hotel is a precise replica of Eureka's nineteenth-century establishment called the Old Town Cairo Hotel. The excellent restaurant can accommodate receptions up to 150.

Grier-Musser Museum, Los Angeles, California

Hotel Carter, Eureka, California (Photograph by Patrick Cudahy)

Grier-Musser Museum
Susan K. Tejada
403 South Bonnie Brae Avenue
Los Angeles, California 90057
(213) 413-1814
Mailing address:
219 South Irving Blvd.
Los Angeles, California 90004

In 1984 this historic house in the Bonnie Brae district of Los Angeles was opened as a museum displaying a collection of antiques and curios, including a nineteenth-century wedding dress. The house is located close to downtown Los Angeles and parking is available. The museum can only accommodate small wedding parties from twenty-five to thirty people and allows no alcoholic beverages except champagne. You must have your own caterer. There are antique costumes and clothing available for rental.

Dunbar House, 1880
Bob and Barbara Costa, Innkeepers
P.O. Box 1375, 271 Jones Street
Murphys, California 95247
(209) 728-2897

This Italianate house is in the historic Gold Country. Murphys is rich with historic buildings and many restaurants.

Churchill Manor
Joanna Guidotti, Innkeeper
485 Brown Street
Napa, California 94559
(707) 253-7733

Churchill Manor is an 1889 three-story mansion listed on the National Register. The manor is situated on an acre of beautifully landscaped grounds and is surrounded by a large verandah. A grand piano is in the music room.

Horton Grand Hotel
Anne Bradford
311 Island Avenue
San Diego, California 92101
(619) 544-1886; 800-999-1886

This is a grand hotel from southern California's glorious 1880s, when guests such as Wyatt Earp and President Benjamin Harrison frequented this elegant establishment. Located adjacent to the Historic Gas Lamp District, the Horton Grand is also minutes from Seaport Village, Sea World, Balboa Park, the Waterfront, and the San Diego Zoo. The elegant Palace Bar and Ida Bailey Restaurant also evoke the rousing days of the Far West in the last century. Weddings of all sizes can be arranged, and the hotel also specializes in arranging romantic honeymoons and anniversary celebrations.

Alamo Square Inn
Wayne M. Corn
719 Scott Street
San Francisco, California 94117
(415) 922-2055

This is a lovely townhouse that hosts weddings up to 150. It is a full-service establishment and everything from the justice of the peace to the wedding cake can be supplied on request.

Archbishop's Mansion Inn
Ralph Woellmer, General Manager
1000 Fulton Street
San Francisco, California 94117
(415) 563-7872

The Archbishop's Mansion Inn is an elegant fifteen-room inn that offers many of the amenities of a larger hotel while maintaining the intimacy of a small inn. It is located in the Alamo Square neighborhood. Up to 100 guests may be accommodated at an indoor reception.

The Gables
4257 Petaluma Hill Road
Santa Rosa, California 95404
(707) 585-7777

This is a lovely bed & breakfast inn in the Wine Country area. Weddings may be held in the garden or in the parlors, or both may be used for a big wedding. A white lattice archway and outdoor furniture can be used for an outdoor wedding.

COLORADO

The Queen Anne Inn
Ann and Chuck Hillestad
2147 Tremont Place
Denver, Colorado 80205
(303) 296-6666

The Queen Anne Inn is a charming 1879 house in the Clements Historic District, a quiet residential area adjacent to both a park and the downtown retail and business center. The inn is beautifully restored, and antiques and period lighting fixtures, together with light chamber music, create a Victorian ambiance. The innkeepers have hosted many weddings and take great pleasure in working with the prospective couple to make the wedding unique. A horse-drawn carriage is available, and the grounds are wonderful for an outdoor ceremony.

Leadville Country Inn
Sid and Judy Clemmer
127 East Eighth Street
Leadville, Colorado 80461
(719) 486-2354

Located in one of the largest historic districts in the country, the inn was built in 1893. The dining room and parlor can accommodate thirty people for an afternoon reception and there is a gazebo for outdoor weddings. A carriage is available for a trip around the town. In winter there is a horse-drawn sleigh. A private candlelight dinner is available for the bride and groom. Cakes and alcoholic beverages can be brought in.

CONNECTICUT

Boulders Inn
Route 45
New Preston, Connecticut 06777
(203) 868-0541

Boulders Inn lies nestled in the Berkshire Hills of northwestern Connecticut overlooking the wooded shores of Lake Waramaug. The large living room, with a handsome Russian samovar in one corner, has a large expanse of windows affording unrestricted views of sunsets over the lake. The private waterfront is excellent for swimming, and canoes, sailboats, rowboats, and paddleboats are provided free of charge. Boulders, an 1895 Dutch Colonial Revival mansion, also has an excellent restaurant. The inn is available for both wedding ceremonies and receptions, and it offers an idyllic setting for both the wedding and honeymoon.

FLORIDA

Lakeside Inn
100 Alexander Street
Mount Dora, Florida 32757
(904) 383-4104
800-556-5016

The Lakeside Inn originally dates from 1883, but it has been restored with a 1930s ambiance. However, in Florida

Boulders Inn, New Preston, Connecticut

that's old. The inn is a large, full-service resort hotel, but it does have a nice, old-fashioned European spirit and is an elegant place for a wedding reception. Daytona Beach is nearby and Disney World and EPCOT Center are forty-two miles away. Mount Dora is a picturesque community with many old homes, and it is known as the "Antiques Capital" of Florida.

The Homeplace, Stuart, Florida

The Homeplace
Jean Bell, Innkeeper
501 Akron Avenue
Stuart, Florida 34994
(407) 220-9148

The Homeplace is a charming 1913 inn located in the historical area of old downtown Stuart. They can accommodate weddings and receptions for up to 100 persons. The ceremony can be performed in front of the fireplace or on the patio, and the inn is decorated for weddings in turn-of-the-century style with ribbons, lace, and greenery indoors and out. Additional decorations are available, including a white arch of flowers or a large flower arrangement floated in the pool. The Homeplace offers a unique Florida-style version of a period wedding.

GEORGIA

Victorian Village
Paul-David Van Atta, General Manager
1841 Hardeman Avenue
Macon, Georgia 31201
(912) 743-3333

The Victorian Village contains four restored Victorian houses dating from 1847 to 1897, and an entire ten-room house can be rented for a wedding. The reception can be catered by the Village's own restaurant, or you can make your own food and beverage arrangements.

ILLINOIS

The Oscar Swan Country Inn
Nina and Hans Heymann
1800 West State Street
Geneva, Illinois 60134
(708) 232-0173

The Oscar Swan Country Inn is a large 1902 Colonial Revival building located on seven acres of land in Fox Valley. It was originally the private home of Oscar and Jessie Swan, and it contains many of their possessions such as European painted furniture. The grounds provide a wonderful backdrop for an outdoor wedding, and the owners assemble tents, do catering, and plan and coordinate the wedding ceremony and reception. They feature European-style receptions that are both casual and sophisticated for fifty to 350 guests.

The Bennett-Curtis House
Sam Van Hook
302 West Taylor Street
Grant Park, Illinois 60940
(815) 465-6025

Set on spacious grounds shaded by hundred-year-old maple trees, The Bennett-Curtis House was built in 1900. A wraparound verandah, furnished with two hundred pieces of antique wicker, also has a porch swing. The house is filled with antiques—cane chairs from Chicago's old Trianon Ballroom, stained glass from a Victorian church, and a collection of music boxes. The unusual thing about this house, lived in and cared for by the Van Hooks, is that it contains a wonderful restaurant. You can also stay overnight. For weddings, both the interior, the verandah, and the grounds can be used for small to huge receptions. The Van Hooks supply antique pews and an altar, and a horse and buggy is available. The grounds have fountains, ornate archways, and over 2,000 plants are put out each spring. The Van Hooks enjoy planning the wedding with the prospective bride and groom and can also advise on such details as music (they can provide a string quartet) and wonderful food. This is a unique and lovely setting for a wedding.

MARYLAND

The Shirley-Madison Inn
Rick Fenstemaker
205 West Madison Street
Baltimore, Maryland 21201
(301) 728-6550

Located in the downtown historic Mt. Vernon neighborhood, this elegant 1880 mansion has a grand English winding stairway, drawing rooms, antiques, stained

The Shirley-Madison Inn, Baltimore, Maryland (Photograph © 1986 Richard Lippenholz)

Oak Bluffs, Massachusetts 02557
(508) 693-4187

The Oak House was built in 1872 from a design by Boston architect Samuel Freeman Pratt. Although there are only ten guest rooms, the public areas are large. If the whole inn is booked, the dining room and porch can be closed off. The owners ask anyone who wishes to have a wedding at the house to reserve at least eight or nine rooms and to arrange their own catering service. However, the owners are happy to recommend local services. The best time for weddings is the off-season from May 10 to June 15 and from September 15 to October 16. The Oak House is closed for the winter. The hotel overlooks the ocean, and the setting is quite romantic.

Monmouth Plantation, Natchez, Mississippi

glass, and a tranquil courtyard. Seated dinners for forty guests, and stand-up receptions for up to 100 guests can be accommodated.

MASSACHUSETTS

The Oak House
Box 299, Seaview Avenue
Martha's Vineyard

MISSISSIPPI

Monmouth Plantation
Marguerite Guercio, Manager, Special Events
36 Melrose Avenue
Natchez, Mississippi 39120
(800) 828-4531

A beautifully restored antebellum mansion on twenty-six acres of romantic grounds, this historic house is now an inn and weddings are a specialty. Several hundred guests can be accommodated on the grounds, and the mansion is large enough for 100 to 150 persons for an indoor wedding. Monmouth Plantation is well known for its fine food that is elegantly presented.

MISSOURI

1909 Depot
Cathy Georgens
Oak and Allen
Bonne Terre, Missouri 63628
(314) 358-5311

This restored train depot is located sixty miles south of St. Louis in the sleepy mining community of Bonne Terre. The south wing of the depot is available for wedding receptions and the second floor has four large suites. There are also horse-drawn carriages available.

Mansion Hill Country Inn
Mansion Hill Drive
Bonne Terre, Missouri 63628
(314) 358-5311

Not far from the 1909 Depot, the Mansion Hill Country Inn is the former estate of the president of the St. Joe Lead Company. It has been extensively restored to a turn-of-the-century ambiance, and it boasts four huge fireplaces. The inn overlooks the surrounding estate situated in the Ozark Mountain foothills, and it features a lake that may be used by the guests.

NEW JERSEY

Grenville Hotel & Restaurant
345 Main Street
Bay Head, New Jersey 08742
(908) 892-3100

This restored 1890 hotel is a block from the ocean in the quaint town of Bay Head. A handsome fireplace, a

The Abbey, Cape May, New Jersey

colonnade, and a crystal chandelier decorate the Victorian lobby. The hotel has a fine restaurant and wines from their own winery. Up to 100 guests may be accommodated.

The Abbey
Jay and Marianne Schatz
Columbia Avenue and Gurney Street
Cape May, New Jersey 08204
(609) 884-4506

Ceremonies can be held in the front parlor for up to thirty-five people, but no food or drink may be brought in. Smoking and children are not allowed.

Columns by the Sea
Barry Rein

1513 Beach Drive
Cape May, New Jersey 08204
(609) 884-2228

This turn-of-the-century mansion with a beautiful view of the ocean can accommodate up to sixty people for wedding and/or receptions and twenty-two to thirty-six people to spend the night. Weddings are not accepted, however, from June 15 through Labor Day, and there is no smoking.

Sea Holly Inn
Christy and Chris Igoe
815 Stockton Avenue
Cape May, New Jersey 08204
(609) 884-6294

The inn will cater a wedding reception. It is required that the inn be booked for two or three nights for a wedding. They can seat twenty-four to twenty-six for a reception, either sit-down or buffet. The "Honeymoon Special" includes a room with an ocean view, wine, breakfast in bed, and tickets for a tour of the area.

White Dove Cottage
Frank Smith, Innkeeper
619 Hughes Street
Cape May, New Jersey 08204
(609) 884-0613

The White Dove Cottage is a Second Empire 1866 house complete with verandah and wicker furniture. It is in the heart of the Cape May historic area, on a quiet gaslit street. The cottage can only accommodate small parties.

Wilbraham Mansion
Pat and Rose Downes
133 Myrtle Avenue
Cape May, New Jersey 08204
(609) 884-2046

This historic mansion in the heart of Cape May hosts both ceremonies and receptions in high Victorian style. Floor-to-ceiling gilded mirrors, crystal chandeliers, and large

Wilbraham Mansion, Cape May, New Jersey

parlors create an elegant, turn-of-the-century atmosphere, and for wedding weekends roses and chamber music abound. A unique feature at the mansion is the indoor pool surrounded by eighty-year-old German stained glass, ferns, and floating candles. The wedding weekend includes a Victorian Bridal Tea on the eve of the ceremony and a Celebration Breakfast the following day.

NEW YORK

The Montauk Club
25 Eighth Avenue

The Montauk Club, Brooklyn, New York

in the grand ballroom. For weddings, the Adelphi specializes in huge, elaborate floral arrangements. Another good thing about a wedding at the Adelphi is that, unlike many hotels, there are no time limits placed on the party, for the hotel will do only one wedding in a day.

Adelphi Hotel, Saratoga Springs, New York (Photograph by Martin Benjamin)

Brooklyn, New York 11217
(718) 638-0800

The Montauk Club was founded in 1889 as an exclusive men's club. Today, it serves the Park Slope community in Brooklyn as a family club. The landmark structure, inspired by Venice's famous Ca d'Oro, was designed in the Venetian Gothic style. There is a variety of private rooms available for wedding receptions.

Adelphi Hotel
Sheila Parkert
365 Broadway
Saratoga Springs, New York 12866
(518) 587-4688

The Adelphi Hotel was built in the days of Saratoga's opulent Victorian past. It has recently been beautifully restored and filled with antiques, evoking the lavishness of Victorian entertaining. The Adelphi also has a unique and imaginative cuisine. The outdoor courtyard with its charming old-fashioned garden is available for the ceremony. Cocktails and hors d'oeuvres are served in the Victorian high style bar and lobby, with dinner following

Chestnut Tree Inn
Cathleen and Bruce DeLuke
9 Whitney Place
Saratoga Springs, New York 12866
(518) 587-8681

This is a small refurbished inn with ten rooms that are filled with Victorian antiques and featuring a wrap-around verandah with wicker furniture. It is available for small weddings and receptions, and there is room for a tent for a small wedding in the yard. It is two blocks from the Canfield Casino and Congress Park, where larger wedding receptions are held.

The Inn at Saratoga
Clair Mahoney
231 Broadway
Saratoga Springs, New York 12866
(518) 583-1890

The inn is a beautifully restored 1880s English-style inn that is right in the heart of Saratoga. The banquet room (the Grosvenor Suite) can accommodate up to 120 people, and the English-style garden is perfect for cocktail receptions. There are also thirty-eight individually decorated guestrooms.

Lombardi Farm
Kathleen Lombardi
34 Locust Grove Road
Saratoga Springs, New York 12866
(518) 587-2074

The Lombardi Farm is a restored Victorian farmhouse on nine acres of land just one and one-half miles from downtown Saratoga Springs. The rooms have beautiful antique pieces, as well as antique stoves. This gentleman's farm is a unique setting for a Saratoga wedding.

OHIO

The Russell-Cooper House
Maureen Tyler
115 East Gambier Street
Mount Vernon, Ohio 43050
(614) 397-8638

This charming inn is nestled in the heart of historic Mount Vernon, known as "America's Hometown." In addition to the antiques-filled guestrooms the Russell-Cooper features a grand ballroom with a hand-painted ceiling, c. 1856, a large sun room, library, formal dining room, and a lovely garden. The Russell-Cooper House is perfect for small indoor or outdoor weddings and receptions, and Maureen and Tim Tyler are enthusiastic about helping the prospective couple arrange all the Victorian details.

PENNSYLVANIA

The Inn at Centre Park
Andrea and Michael Smith
730 Centre Avenue
Reading, Pennsylvania
(215) 374-8557

The Russell-Cooper House, Mount Vernon, Ohio

An 1877 granite Gothic house, the mansion has wonderful stained-glass panels, carved wood, Moravian tiles, and ornate plaster. Weddings have become a specialty, and the innkeepers tailor each event to be what the bride wants it to be. They do it all: flowers, catering, music, and wedding cakes. The inn can accommodate comfortably receptions up to 125 people.

RHODE ISLAND

Block Island Resorts
The 1661 Inn and Hotel Manisses
Joan Abrams
Block Island, Rhode Island 02807
(401) 466-2063, 466-2421

Block Island is a small, windswept parcel of land that is thirteen miles from the mainland. The whole island is a wonderfully romantic setting. The Hotel Manisses is an 1870 Victorian hotel in the only town on the island, and it was once known as one of the best hotels in the East. The Abrams family saved it from destruction in 1972 and have lovingly restored it. A vine-covered porch and a mansard

The Inn at Centre Park, Reading, Pennsylvania

roof and belvedere distinguish the exterior, and the interior features antiques, ceiling fans, and wide Eastlake-style beds. It also has baseboard heating and Jacuzzis. The 1661 Inn guest house is of an earlier Colonial period. Both hotels are on the National Register and are wonderfully romantic places for a wedding and have lovely gardens. Block Island is about an hour's ferry ride from Rhode Island's mainland.

Sea Fare Inn
Anna Karousos
3352 East Main Road, Rt. 138
Portsmouth, Rhode Island 02871
(401) 683-0577

This five-star restaurant is located in an 1887 Victorian mansion containing six separate dining rooms and a ballroom. Master chef George Karousos prepares wonderful food based on a philosophy of cooking known as Archestratios-Epicurean cuisine. His wife, Anna, has restored the mansion with antiques, rich fabrics, and scenic oil paintings. The ten acres surrounding the inn bloom with the chef's herb and vegetable garden and a variety of fruit trees. A very elegant setting for a reception.

Sea Fare Inn, Portsmouth, Rhode Island

VIRGINIA

Morrison House
Sylvie Farbstein
116 South Alfred Street
Alexandria, Virginia 22314
(703) 684-3961

This small hotel has a European charm. Period decor and excellent cuisine make it a good choice for rehearsal dinners or bridal luncheons up to forty-six guests, and receptions up to 180 people.

WASHINGTON

The Abel House
Victor J. Reynolds
117 Fleet Street South
Montesano, Washington 98563
(206) 249-6002

This 1908 house features a Tiffany chandelier, an English country dining room, and a library with a fireplace. Available for weddings, the house is surrounded by lovely grounds. The small town of Montesano is near Lake Sylvia and the Tall Ships project, Ocean Shores beaches, and the Olympic National Parks rain forest. From the northern edge of the Olympic peninsula, Victoria, British Columbia, is only a ferry cruise away.

WASHINGTON, D.C.

Morrison-Clark Hotel
Massachusetts Avenue and 11th Street, N.W.
Washington, D.C. 20001
(202) 898-1200; (800) 332-7898

The Morrison-Clark is a historic inn that comprises two grand townhouses completed in 1864 and enlarged in 1876. In 1917, a two-story verandah was added. There are several dining rooms and a courtyard available for receptions and dinners up to 125. The furnishings are an elegant mix of Victorian and classic styles. The hotel is quite accessible to National airport, the train station, and most of D.C.

WEST VIRGINIA

Yesterdays Ltd.
Carlyn Smith, William H. Fields
827 Main Street
Wheeling, West Virginia 26003
(304) 233-2003

Yesterdays Ltd. is the management name for a group of bed & breakfasts that include an 1895 townhouse and an 1896 mansion in the oldest historic area of Wheeling, which is known for its rowhouses perched along the bluffs of the Ohio River. These houses are a few blocks away from Victorian Wheeling, a city rich in Victorian history and architecture. It is a riverboat town, and you can still ride the Valley Voyager, a paddlewheeler. Fields Hall Performing Arts Center is also available for weddings. Fields Hall features stained-glass windows, columns, and balconies. List House, a Victorian mansion nearby, is available for rehearsal dinners.

Old Rittenhouse Inn and Le Chateau Boutin, Bayfield, Wisconsin

WISCONSIN

Old Rittenhouse Inn
and *Le Chateau Boutin*
Mary and Jerry Phillips, Innkeepers
Contact: Debra Carlson
P.O. Box 584
Bayfield, Wisconsin 54814
(715) 779-5111

Ceremonies and receptions up 125 people are arranged by the innkeeper, Jerry Phillips, who is also licensed to perform the wedding ceremony. The special small-wedding package includes one night's lodging with champagne, sweets, a fireplace, and a second guest room for friends. The marriage ceremony, flowers, and dinner for four with a wedding torte, and breakfast, complete the package.

Specialties

One of the most appealing aspects of planning a Victorian-style wedding is the opportunity it gives to personalize such wedding items as announcements, invitations, and thank-you notes. One would, of course, dispense with printed matchbooks and other modern notions. There are many companies today that reproduce color art for making decoupage and other handcrafts. With the advent of chromolithography, Victorian printers were able to produce wonderfully sentimental bits of colored paper. It was avidly collected in scrapbooks and thus became known as "paper scrap." Today, in the form of stickers, it can be used to create charming items. For example, a young lady we know had her wedding invitation printed in the usual way. The prospective bride and her attendants then applied a colored sticker to the outside and inside to make a colorful and unusual wedding invitation. Another item that has made a comeback is a reproduction of a wedding certificate from the nineteenth century. These make delightful wedding, shower, and anniversary gifts.

And Tat's Tat
Dottie Main
1021 Heard Drive S.E.
Huntsville, Alabama 35803
(205) 883-6993

Dottie Main takes stationery items (thank-you notes, wedding invitations printed by her engraver, etc.) and creates custom designs with paint and with an old method of using thread for decorative purposes known as tatting. Her designs have a delicate, old-fashioned appearance. She will consult by mail or phone.

Carrol Rose
P.O. Box 90393
Austin, Texas 78709
(512) 892-1295; 800-462-6720

Carrol Rose has two marriage certificates: "Victorian Ladies," which is reproduced from a 1901 marriage, and "Flowers and Butterflies," which is a contemporary design. The certificates are produced on 100% acid-free paper, and they are available in both English and Spanish. You may also order the certificate filled out with calligraphy if desired.

Victorian Certificates
2035 St. Andrews Circle
Carmel, Indiana 46032
(317) 844-5648

This company specializes in reproductions of engraved certificates from the 1800s. Sentimental Victorian couples proudly displayed their marriage certificates, which came in many styles, including the sweetly sentimental or the type with biblical admonishments. These beautifully reproduced certificates have 4" x 6" cut-out to hold a photograph of the bride and groom. This is also a lovely gift for an anniversary. With the addition of calligraphy for the names and date, a charming Victorian-style keepsake is re-created.

Victorian House
128 North Longwood Street
Rockford, Illinois 61107
(815) 963-3351; 608-362-1266

This company reproduces certificates from the nineteenth century, including birth, wedding, and family-register certificates. One antique wedding certificate from the collection of the Dallas County Heritage Society has sepia-tint roses on a landscape background. Another from the Missouri Historical Society has spaces for photographs of the bride and groom, and there is one with a religious theme from California. The catalog includes Victorian-style picture hangers to use when framing the certificate.

Morning Star Publishers, Inc.
P.O. Box 6388
Destin, Florida 32541
(904) 837-5011

Original designs that are Victorian-inspired include place cards, calling cards, note cards, and a Victorian wedding album.

The Paper Potpourri
P.O. Box 5575
Portland, Oregon 97228-5575

This company has a delightful potpourri of paper items that inspire projects or make charming small gifts that would be appropriate for gifts to the bridesmaids or for shower presents or favors. *Romantic Memory Pieces* is a booklet that shows how to organize memorabilia into shadow boxes, etc., and is very popular for creating wedding-memory artifacts. The reproduction fans are often used in lieu of traditional bridal bouquets as well as gifts. The Paper Potpourri catalog is $2.00.

Diane M. Smoler
12 Perry Lane
Ridgefield, Connecticut 06877
(203) 438-6195

Ms. Smoler is an artist who creates porcelain dolls for individual clients. Her specialty is creating a doll wearing an exact duplicate of the bridal dress, or one in authentic nineteenth-century wedding attire. A former fashion designer, Ms. Smoler's eye for detail is excellent. She will create the doll from the bride's dress as a wedding keepsake or later as an anniversary gift. Her dolls are delicately handpainted, hair individually styled, and meticulous attention is given to each detail of the costume. Even the underwear and shoes are exact replicas. Only the finest fabrics and trims are used, and the bridal doll will be luxuriously attired from head to toe, including her bouquet. Ms. Smoler works from photographs and newspaper accounts, when available. She even includes a miniaturized copy of the wedding invitation and a brass plate with the bride's name and wedding date is affixed to the stand. These exquisite dolls are for very special presents and serious collectors.

An example of the delightful reproductions of engraved marriage certificates available from Victorian Certificates.

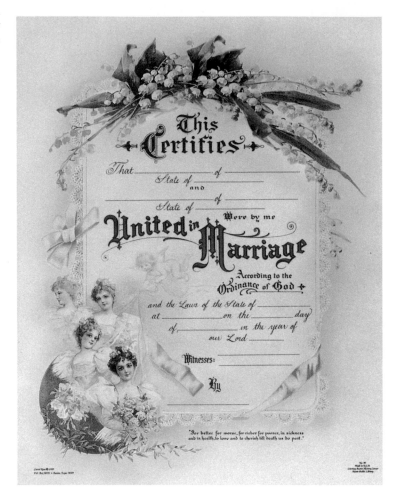

can either choke when eating it or suffer dire consequences later. A nice alternative to the traditional rice is dried fragrant rose petals and birdseed, nicely packaged by this firm. The petals and birdseed make a romantic send-off at the church or at the reception, are not harmful to birds, and leave a pleasant clutter. "Wedding Throws" are about $10.00 at many wedding-specialty stores, or contact the company for a store near you.

"Wedding Throws"
Mullen and Fitzmaurice
51 South Street
Hingham, Massachusetts 02043
(617) 749-1320

Sometimes a departure from tradition is a good thing. It has been discovered that the rice traditionally thrown at weddings is very harmful to birds. They eat the rice and

Helpful Publications

Nineteenth Century
Victorian Society of America
219 South 6th Street
Philadelphia, Pennsylvania 19106
(215) 627-4252

Nineteenth Century is a quarterly publication included with the membership fee to the Victorian Society of $25.00 for an individual and $30.00 for a household. The Victorian Society of America is devoted to the appreciation and preservation of America's nineteenth-century heritage. Membership also includes information about local chapters and news about symposiums.

Victorian Homes
P.O. Box 61
Millers Falls, Massachusetts 01349
(413) 659-3785

This is a magazine about nineteenth- and early twentieth-century architecture, decoration, and lifestyles. Each issue features restored homes and apartments, historic houses, Victorian gardening, decorating tips, and techniques. There are occasional articles about Victorian-style weddings. Articles on bed & breakfasts and travel are regularly featured, and they are often places where Victorian wedding re-creations are held. The subscription cost is $18.00 for six issues per year.

Vintage Clothing
Published by Hobby House Press

900 Frederick Street
Cumberland, Maryland 21502
(301) 759-3770

This is a magazine (6 issues per year for $19.95) for the collector of vintage clothing. There are articles about caring for collections, styles of the past, and helpful ads for shows and places where one can buy antique clothing.

Past Patterns
P.O. Box 7587
Grand Rapids, Michigan 49502-1014
(616) 245-9456

Past Patterns, listed in our dress listing, also offers a varied list of books that have to do with period costume, sewing techniques, etc. Just a few are: *The Art of Tying the Cravat, Corsets & Crinolines*, and *Children's Clothes since 1750*. A full list is published on the back of the Victorian and Edwardian Catalog ($3.00), or you can write or call about the subject that is of particular interest to you.

Zwemmer Art Booksellers
24 Litchfield Street
London WC2H 9NJ
England

For very specialized books on costume history, write for a free catalog.

Conclusion

By the time you have picked the place for your wedding and considered what you and the bridal party will wear, you will most likely have acquired a lot of knowledge about the Victorian era. But you must remember that your guests have not! For their Victorian-style wedding in San Francisco, Lynne Jackson and Paul Watson sent letters to those who replied that they would be attending the wedding. The letters gave some suggestions for places to rent period clothing and names and addresses of places to stay in the area. If some of the guests are planning to wear period clothing it is only fair to let all the guests know. Because a Victorian wedding re-creation is unique, it is in the spirit of Victorian etiquette not to let it be a surprise.

Because your wedding will be different you are free to do many things not commonly part of the wedding reception. You may wish to add some Victorian entertainment: music, a magic act, something for the children. While these activities were not part of the Victorian wedding reception, they would be fun for today.

There are a few cautions. Nothing will ruin the Victorian ambiance of the event as much as video cameras and incessant picture taking. If you are sending out a letter, you might ask guests not to take photographs during the ceremony. Most weddings and graduations these days resemble a presidential press conference with flashes going off and the video camera man blocking the view of the guests at the ceremony. Photographs should be relegated to their proper place: a sitting after the ceremony and before the receiving line. But it should be fairly brief. You might want to look around for a photographer who takes photographs with an old camera or can create the sepia-tone look of old photos.

Loud, modern music will, of course, ruin the atmosphere immediately. If you are having a wedding breakfast there is no need for music. However, a string quartet or other small group would be a charming asset. Often a nearby music school or college will have students available to play. For dancing, you could have recorded music made up of waltzes and genteel ragtime if live music is unavailable. But for just one afternoon or evening it is not too much to ask your guests to forfeit the "Twist and Shout" kind of music. Most guests will likely be very grateful.

Most important: *enjoy your wedding*. You are celebrating the beginning of a long and happy life together, and your guests should feel that happiness radiating from the bridal couple out to the entire wedding party.

One Final Word

Although the references used to develop this book have been faithfully listed, some call for an additional word of credit for the depth of information they contributed.

Both *Brides and Bridals*, written in 1872 by John Cordy Jeaffreson, and *To Love and To Cherish*, written in 1989 by Linda Otto Lipsett, gave the many superstitions about the best days and the best months for a wedding. Monsarrat's book also contained some interesting superstitions.

Catherine Zimmerman's book, *The Bride's Book: A Pictorial History of American Bridal Dress*, not only mentioned the frontier bride and her shawl, but she also had newspaper accounts from the Midwest of dresses worn by brides and their mothers.

As for the bridegroom's attire, although the correspondence columns in the ladies' magazines were full of advice and "rules," *Costume for Births, Marriages and Deaths* by Phyllis Cunnington and Catherine Lucas had the authoritative word on men's fashions direct from *The Tailor and Cutter, The Minister's Gazette,* and the *West End Gazette of Fashion.*

All of the quotes from Queen Victoria's journals and letters are from Christopher Hibbert's wonderful book. These were the principal source of information on her engagement and wedding, although *British Royal Brides* by Josy Argy and Wendy Hicks contributed many additional details that helped to round out the story. Even a trip to the old newspaper library in London didn't turn up any accounts of the event.

Consuelo Vanderbilt's wedding, on the other hand, was described in detail in many old newspapers, as well as in her book *The Glitter and the Gold. Fortune's Children* by Arthur T. Vanderbilt II was the source for the description of the money settlement in the marriage contract that was signed during the interval in the service when the bride and groom followed the British tradition of stepping into the vestry to sign the register.

Perhaps the most cherished reference of all was a book no longer in print. *The Marriage of Diamonds and Dolls* by Mary Lewis and Dorothy Dignam had precise descriptions of everything, including the trousseau, the jewels, and the wedding, organized and presented decade by decade. Without exaggeration, many of the fine points on all aspects of Victorian weddings of the past that we were able to include in this book came to our attention because two authors, who preceded us by more than forty years, had thoroughly done their research.

Bibliography

Books

Argy, Josy and Wendy Rickes. *British Royal Brides*. London, Vancouver, David & Charles, 1975.

Balsan, Consuelo Vanderbilt. *The Glitter and the Gold*. New York: Harper & Brothers Publishers, 1952.

Cannon, Poppy and Patricia Brooks. *The Presidents' Cookbook*. New York: Funk & Wagnalls, 1968.

Cross, Wilbur and Ann Novotny. *White House Weddings*. New York: David McKay Company, Inc., 1967.

Cunnington, Phillis and Catherine Lucas. *Costume for Births, Marriages & Deaths*. London: Adam & Charles Black, 1972.

Dick's Society Letter-Writer For Ladies. New York: Dick & Fitzgerald, 1884.

Filippini, Allessandro. *The Table: How to Buy Food, How to Cook It, and How to Serve It*. New York, Charles L. Webster & Co., 1889.

Hibbert, Christopher. *Queen Victoria in Her Letters and Journals*. New York: Viking, 1985.

Hooker, Richard J. *Food and Drink in America: A History*. Indianapolis/New York, 1981.

Jeaffreson, John Cordy. *Brides and Bridals*. Vol. I., London: Hurst and Blackett, Publishers, 1872.

King, Caroline B. Introduction by Jill Gardner. *Victorian Cakes*. Aris/Berkeley.

Kingsland, Mrs. Burton. *Etiquette for All Occasions*. New York: Doubleday, Page and Company, 1902.

Lewis, Mary E. and Dorothy Dignam. *The Marrige of Diamonds and Dolls*. New York: H.L. Lindquist Publications, 1947.

Lipsett, Linda Otto. *To Love & To Cherish; Brides Remembered*. The Quilt Digest Press, San Francisco, 1989.

Longstreet, Mrs. Abby Buchanan. *Good Form: Weddings Formal and Informal*. New York: Frederick A. Stokes Company, 1891.

Longstreet, Mrs. Abby Buchanan. *Social Etiquette of New York*. New York: D. Appleton and Company, 1892.

Monsarrat. *And the Bride Wore…, The Story of the White Wedding*. New York: Dodd, Mead & Company, 1973.

Nicholson, Shirley. *A Victorian Household: Based on the Diaries of Marion Sambourne*. London: Barrie & Jenkins, 1988.

Packer, Jane. *Flowers for All Seasons*. New York: Fawcett Columbine, 1989.

Parloa, Miss Maria. *Miss Parloa's Kitchen Companion Illustrated*. Boston, Estes and Laurist, 1887.

Sherwood, Mrs. John. *Manners and Social Usages*. New York: Harper & Brothers Publishers, 1897.

Smith, Marie. *Entertaining in the White House*. Washington, D.C.: Acropolis Books, 1967.

Vanderbilt, Arthur T., II. *Fortune's Children: The Fall of the House of Vanderbilt*. New York: William Morrow and Company, Inc., 1989.

Victorian Shopping. Harrod's 1895 Catalogue. New York: St. Martin's Press: 1972.

Warwick, Christopher. *Two Centuries of Royal Weddings*. New York: Dodd, Mead & Company, 1980.

Wason, Betty. *Cooks, Gluttons & Gourmets: A History of Cookery*. Garden City, New York: Doubleday & Company, Inc., 1962.

Wells, Richard A. *Decorum, A Practical Treatise on Etiquette and Dress*. New York, Cincinnati, Portland, Atlanta: Union Publishing House, 1886.

Young, John H. *Our Deportment*. Harrisburg, Pennsylvania: Pennsylvania Publishing Co. Detroit, Michigan: F.B. Dickerson & Co. Hamilton, Ontario: 1880.

Zimmerman, Catherine S. *The Bride's Book: A Pictorial History of American Bridal Dress*. New York: Arbor House, 1985.

Periodicals
Girl's Own Paper, The: 1887
Godey's Lady's Book: 1861, 1864, 1872.
Gourmet: "The Lore of the Wedding Cake" by Evan Jones. June 1983.
Grand Rapids Herald (Michigan): May 12, 1897.
Harper's Bazar: 1882, 1883, 1885, 1886, 1890, 1891, 1898.
Harper's Weekly: 1886.
Illustrated London News
Ladies' Home Journal: 1890, 1891, 1892, 1894, 1899, 1902, 1906.
New York Daily Tribune, The: November 7, 1895.
New York Times, The: November 7, 1895.
Peterson's Magazine: 1858, 1860, 1864.
Sunday Magazine, 1883.
Westporter (Connecticut): October 29, 1881, May 14, 1881, September 24, 1881, December 24, 1881.
Young Ladies' Journal, The: 1872.